DEDICATION

This book is dedicated to you! You are the reason I write...

CONTENTS

Acknowledgments   I

Prologue   II

The ABC's Of Success

1	Welcome	Pg 1
2	My Story	Pg 5
3	For The Committed People	Pg 13
4	Let's Get It Started	Pg 17
5	Don't Reinvent The Wheel	Pg 21
6	What Are You Going To Learn	Pg 25
7	The ABC's Of Success	Pg 31
8	Mindset	Pg 39
9	Goal Achieving	Pg 47
10	Time Management	Pg 57
11	The Story Of Some People	Pg 71
12	Watch What Happens	Pg 79
13	Associations	Pg 85
14	Energy	Pg 95
15	Commitments	Pg 105
16	Put Yourself First	Pg 111
17	Intuition	Pg 115
18	C.H.O.I.C.E.	Pg 119
19	Create Your Goal	Pg 125
20	Time to reflect	Pg 135

ACKNOWLEDGMENTS

Thank you God, for giving me purpose! In my quest for wisdom, and knowledge, it was You who allowed me to understand how important my life really is to You. I love You more than anything, and anyone, anywhere! You are my Creator, my one and only God, my true Father and the love of my life, forever, always and for all eternity.

I want to give a special acknowledgment to ValleyPoint Church. When I needed a place to rest, you invited me in and gave me a place to call home. In your love, I understood what it meant to be significant. In your embrace, I understood what it meant to grow in my relationship with God. You are a significant part of my family now and I love our relationship.

To my Mom. If it wasn't for you, I would not have been introduced to the greatest mentor I have ever had the privilege of learning from. You have always been the one person who knew exactly what I needed in my life. Your love is unconditional, and because of that, I understand what it means to love, unconditionally. You are the brightest light I've ever known on this earth. Thank you for everything you have ever done and everything you have ever been for me. I couldn't ask for a better mom.

Dad, I get it! This moment is the happiest moment of my life. Not everyone does, but I get you. You have grown so much in your life. I'm so proud of you and I am truly thankful to be your son. Keep being you, you do it the best! Keep being the best Pop Pop you can be, they need you!

My brother. It was you, who always had confidence in me. I always felt it, and I always appreciate it, to this very day. I hope that you know how much you are loved! I miss you, I love you, and I pray for you. Be well!

My wife, you came into my life at the moment I needed you! God knows we need each other! I need you more and more every day. I love you more and more every day, and I appreciate you more and more every day! Thank you for always supporting me, and making me believe that I can do anything! We have both grown so much, and I'm looking forward to continuing our journey, till death do us part.

My children. My love for you is beyond anything you could ever imagine. Your support, confidence, and belief in me is unparalleled. I've been so blessed, by each and every one of you. My life, without any of you, would not be exactly the way it should be. I love you, I love you, I love you! Be who you were born to be!

To Frank, my oldest and dearest friend. We may not be together on earth, but we are connected in spirit. Thank you for giving me all that you had to give. I felt your love, I knew your friendship, and I appreciate the gift. You are gone, but you are definitely not forgotten, ever. Until we meet again!

Brendon Burchard, the man who showed me how to live, how to love, and how to matter! I thank God for your life! You don't know me, but you matter more than you could possibly know. Because you lived, because you loved, because you mattered, I started living, loving, and mattering! My thankfulness for your golden ticket cannot be valued in dollars. Your life is a priceless gift to many, and an invaluable series of moments that transformed who I am. Thank you!

Last, but not least, I want to acknowledge you, the reader. If it wasn't for you, I would have no reason to write. You give me purpose! My love for you is also true. I may not know you personally, but I love you just the same. If we all did for each other, what you do for me, this world would be a much more loving place. I only ask one thing of you. Allow me to love you, inspire you, motivate you, and empower you. If you do that, everything else will take care of itself…

I love you all, wholeheartedly, unconditionally, and beyond measure.

Prologue

There are a few specific moments in my life that, I believe, had a profound impact on where I am today. There have also been many leaders who have served an amazing purpose in my life, I would love to personally thank them all, but there just aren't enough pages in this book to do so. If you are a leader, just know that I thank you and I value your life with tremendous respect.

That being said, there is one leader who I met as a child that came back into my life as I began writing Your Journey Of Being. He is the *only* one who has ever given me a level of clarity that no one else could ever provide. He is the one who helped me to reach the level of personal success that I have reached. Everyone else that I've mentioned and thanked has helped me reach the peak. Only He has helped me reach beyond the peak to a place of infinite possibility where a completely new realm of life exists. He's not the typical personal development leader. He's not the guy you see on stage, in the media, on the cover of success magazine or anywhere else. He is the most humble, understated, and misunderstood leader you could ever meet. His work is underappreciated, misquoted, ridiculed, and currently banned in 52 countries! If you have the privilege of owning His books, reading them, and understanding them, you will gain a level of knowledge that no one else can give you. He is true brilliance!

He doesn't put His name on any of the books He has written because He is so humble, He doesn't demand recognition. Clearly, He lives by one principle and one law, love. His doors are left unlocked, despite the fact that He owns more than you could imagine. Anything He has is yours, you only need to ask. If you are hungry, He will feed you, thirsty you can drink as much as you need. His wealth is beyond measure and far surpasses anything that humans could value, which is why you don't see Him on the list of the world's wealthiest people. The gifts He gives me are priceless, and I wouldn't hesitate to say that if you needed His only child, He would give Him to you if it would save your life. That is just who He is, and I am blessed to be able to call Him my friend and my Father. I'm excited to introduce you to Him and share with you, what I believe, are His words. He is God.

Along with His other books, I believe He is actually the co-writer of this book because of how He inspires me to write. He doesn't want credit, but I give Him all the credit. I could not write what I put into words without His spirit guiding me. You'll likely see a transition from who I used to be, to who I am now by the time you are done reading this book series, and I hope the same happens for you. I'm not going to tell you that a transition from who you are today, to who you want to become will occur just because you read this book. I do believe it's possible though, that a complete transformation may happen in your life as a result of the words He has spoken. This book was inspired by the words of God. I love hearing His words, and I hope that the way I share what He says, brings more love into your life.

While I was beginning to gain a clarity and understanding about life, during my writing process, I was completely open to any messages God was sending me. I began to notice that what I wanted to share with the world was based solidly in the words of God. I didn't know it at first, but now I believe it wholeheartedly. It was His wisdom that guided me during the writing of this book and I used my unique voice to put it into my own words. Because I was open to the knowledge that was available, I understood what He was telling me. All I needed to do was transcribe the wisdom, in my own unique writing style, and use it to serve. I'm so thankful that I have been given the greatest gifts I could ever ask for in life. I am blessed beyond belief, and my hope is that when you finish reading this book, you will be too. You can be, if you choose to be.

When I set out to write Your Journey Of Being, I had no idea of the journey I was embarking on myself. Where I began, and where I ended up, was not where I would have expected to be. I hope that you experience the same level of surprise as you read these books as I experienced while writing these books.

This is not your typical "How to be successful" book series. Although this book starts out as most personal development, goal setting, time management books do because it is the foundation of everything else you will learn, as the series advances, so will your level of understanding about how life works! I don't know what level you are at in life, so in order to be sure I'm offering the very best help, I intentionally started at base camp. I can confidently say, this series is unlike any other book series you have ever read. The concepts are deceptively simple for a reason, but the depth of wisdom comes from a place of true brilliance, and that's not from me, but from God Himself. Keeping life simple is one of the best kept secrets around. It just might be the key to your success!

As you climb this extraordinary mountain, you will realize something amazing. Intuitively, because I've been up the mountain many times, I can skillfully navigate the terrain you are about to embark on. With that said, I want you to think of me as your success Sherpa. As you climb your mountain of success, I'll be there to guide your path. When you reach the peak, I'll be with you, excited to see your arms raised in victory! I'm here, with you and for you!

The goal, when I set my mind to writing this, was to take everything I had learned over the years and condense it down into one extraordinary personal development, goal achievement and success focused guidebook. The idea was to boil down what it truly takes to succeed and display the wisdom in such a way that everyone could benefit from this work. What I didn't know is that my plans were my own, but that God had much greater plans for this book.

The first challenge was to write a book that would walk someone who never opened a personal development book, from the very beginning of what it takes to succeed in life, to the peak of what's possible so they can see life from a new perspective. The second challenge was to write it in such a way that the contents would also be fresh and insightful for a seasoned self-help expert. I believe I accomplished that goal.

I didn't plan to write this entire series, I just kept writing, because the level of wisdom I obtained was ever increasing. When I discovered something along the way, during my writing journey, I had the desire to immediately share it with others so they can benefit from the knowledge. You see, I am a work in progress, just like you. As life evolved for me, so did the words you read in these pages. The clarity that evolved during the writing process took me to a whole new level of understanding. As one book was written, the next would reveal itself.

Throughout my life, I've had the privilege of learning from the top leaders in personal development. They are the best writers, speakers, and trainers this world has to offer. I'd like to thank them all, but that would fill a book itself. I encourage you to dive into personal development like it was the fountain of youth. Soak it in, feel the words and allow them to absorb you. Be a sponge for knowledge, but don't ever have the desire to know it all.

I hope that this book, in some way, changes your life for the better! More importantly, I hope that this book, in some way, changes the world for the better. If you are willing to do your part to make that happen, I believe, together we can literally transform the world! However, that is going to take one intentional way of being from both of us. I'm willing to do my part, and I expect nothing in return.

During my journey to where I am today, and who I am today, I got off track many times. The path I chose has not been an easy one. To say that I have been in some pretty dark places in my life would be an understatement. To sum up those times I would use words like unfulfilled, dissatisfied, discontent and frustrated. Not unhappy, just really unclear about what I wanted for my life. I found myself living a life that was full of negative disbeliefs about what really mattered.

I honestly had no idea what mattered, and no matter how hard I searched for success, it eluded me. Fulfillment, personal success, and inner peace were three things I had to struggle to find daily. I lived in darkness, and didn't allow my light to shine.

Thankfully, I was protected and guided during that time. The choices I made during those years led to much more of an eeny, meenie, miney, moe, close my eyes and go for it type of action. I didn't follow The Light that was guiding me. I shut out the possibility that there was a God who loved me, knew what was best for me, and wanted the best for me. Even if He was talking to me, I certainly wasn't listening.

The guidance I was being given, wasn't clear to me at that time in my life. It wasn't until I looked back, years later, and realized what He was doing for me that I truly got His plan. I don't know what the future holds, and at this point, it makes no difference to me. I am, exactly where I want to be in my life. I have God to thank for that fact!

My desire for you is to help you discover true personal success and complete fulfillment in every moment. Personal success is different for everyone, which makes the challenge of writing a book that helps you, all the more challenging. The fact is, I don't have any idea what matters to you, and I certainly don't know what personal success is for you. I do have a confession to make though. I know someone who has been watching you, and He does know what you want and need! Creepy right!

I had a lot of help writing this book. When I would sit down to write, I would open my arms, invite the spirit of God to speak through me, and use me as the writing implement to share His wisdom. I believe that He did that for me, and for you. He spoke the words and I wrote them down. That voice in my head that formed each sentence took signals from my heart which heard the words.

I never understood the leaders of my life who would say that you need to have your physical, emotional, mental, and spiritual life in order before you will feel successful. I understood all of them, except for the spiritual requirement. I resisted it, and therefore, I never felt successful.

Within the pages of this book, you are going to discover some new concepts. I hope these chapters help you to find clarity, if anything is out of focus for you right now. The purpose of this book is not to force you to believe anything or to prove any point. I simply set out to bring into existence, The Light of hope that you may need or want in your life.

Whether you are a believer in God, higher spiritual powers, a divine being, universal forces, or in nothing at all, makes no difference. The honest reality of the words you are about to read is the fact that they are inspired by my life's journey. I have had a lot of mentors, coaches, spiritual leaders, opinions, proof, scientific facts and simple beliefs to go on. The truth is, I don't know what to believe, I only know what I believe. In order to clarify my desire for what you are about to read, I need to highlight a simple truth so it does not get misconstrued during your reading. I believe, that your belief is the only thing that matters.

The truth I need to clarify is this: No matter what you believe, doesn't matter for this information to make a profound difference in your life. The word I use in this book series is God. I also use the word He, The Light, His, Him, etcetera. You can interchange those words to suit your personal needs, if the word God is not what you use. I get it, it was a weird word for me to use for many years too. I use that word to keep consistency in this writing. Feel free to adjust how you use The Word to suit your needs. Whatever you do, don't let a simple noun stop you from reading. It doesn't mean anything anyway, but it does matter!

I believe that God is guiding me, right now, as I write these very words. If you are open to the possibility that something may be guiding your life to read these words, then keep reading. You may discover something in this work that lays the foundation for a completely new belief system in your life.

Be open to the possibility that this book was written for you, by God. I was! When I was writing the words, I was open to the possibility that He was guiding me. The fact is, I'm open to wisdom and I listen with an open heart. I also have an unwavering desire to help other people. I consider myself a servant leader, and if this book serves you, then that makes me joyously successful! I'm here, to serve, based on His plan for my life. If that plan consists of me leading you to the place He wants you to be, then I feel like I'm serving my purpose well.

I poured out to you all that I could in these pages and I hope these words flood your heart with love and wisdom, because that is my intentional purpose for setting out to complete this work. To help you live your life with passion, purpose, and possibility in every moment. I believe we can all do that, if we learn to love His wisdom!

Because you haven't solidified these concepts in your own mind yet, I realize that what I'm about to say may not make sense. Don't worry, by the time you finish reading this book series, these ideas will not only make sense, they may in fact begin to form a new belief system in your life. All you need to know right now is that I just want to love, create love and inspire love. With that said; I am, a light of possibility, and in this moment, I choose to be!

If you are ready to be who you were born to be, then let's start being.

Love….

Tom

Welcome

Does your life have a design? If you don't know, I'll give you the answer. Yes, it does! However, you must answer the question, is it your design or someone else's? You may be fulfilling the purpose of someone else's design of how they want their life to look, and using you in the process. The fact is, you have to know the purpose of your life, so you can design your life around that purpose. But how do you design your life if you don't know your purpose? Within the pages of this book, we are going to explore some unique ideas to help you identify your purpose, inspire you, ignite your passion and design the exact life you want to live! My goal, is for you to know every moment of every day how to live your most desired life!

Have you ever looked around and realized that everything in the world has a design? Take a minute, everything you see serves a purpose. When you think about the process of design, here are the stages. Identify a need. Figure out what purpose will be served through the unique design. Rough out a plan by identifying what will be necessary in order to match the need with the design.

Refine, refine, refine until your design is exactly what you want it to be in order to fulfill the purpose. That's my job, to help you discover your purpose and passionately live that life, by design! I am, a life design expert, and it's my job to help you design your life!

Welcome to the ABC's Of Success. You are on your journey to having and being anything you want in your life. I'm so excited for you right now because I know what lies ahead. I know what is going to be introduced to you on this journey. I mapped out this journey for you and I really want you to experience it the way that it was designed. The way that you get the most out of your experience is to not just read this book but use the workbook style pages that are provided. Use the information and do the work because when you read this book and do the work you will be inspired, you will create, you will be alive again in a way that you've never been alive before.

I don't know where you are right now, you may be wildly successful already, and that's great. I want you to be even more successful. You might just be in a place where you have no idea what you want for your life and, if that's you, I'm sorry that you're in that place right now but I'm not going to allow you to stay there because you matter to me. Your success matters to me. What you want matters to me and I hope it matters to you.

You see, if I don't help you get what you want than I'm not doing my job. If you're not on your way to living the life that you really want to live, after you're done with this book, I'm not doing my job. I hope that you take this book seriously. Have fun, but take it seriously, because I did. I had a lot of fun writing this book for you. I had a lot of fun envisioning it, designing it, creating it, writing it, and then sharing it with you. I did it for you. I also took it seriously, because your life matters. You only get one shot at this, so I want to teach you how to live life to the fullest.

The reason I wrote this book is because I want you to experience life at your peak, in every moment. I want you to experience what I experience because life at its highest level is an amazing life. I know that you might not have everything you want in your life right now. You might not have the external things that more money can buy. I also understand that you might not be as happy as you want to be in your life right now. In fact, you may be missing many of the internal feelings you desire.

I understand that and you know what, I was there, I've been through this, and I promise you that you now have a book that is unlike any other book that you have ever read in your life. My hope is that you get a thousand times the value that you paid for this book. I hope that your life becomes better than you could possibly imagine. I hope you get anything you want, because that is my job. That's my envisionment for you. That's what I want for your life, I want you to live life at the peak with me, so let's do it together.

I'm going to show you what my journey was and I'm going to show you where I was and how I got to where I am today, so that you can be assured that I can help you. The first thing I want to do is tell you a little bit of my story. I want you to understand that I didn't always live this life of pure joy and excitement, personal success, and extraordinary fulfillment. I didn't always live at the peak of what's possible for my life. I had to learn it and it took me a long time. I failed and I struggled and I failed again and I struggled again and I just kept going and I kept learning and I kept trusting that I was on the right track.

I knew where I wanted to be in my life and I finally got there. Once I reached the point in my life that I said, "This is it. I've lived it, I've experienced it, I know how to get there and now I can show other people." That's when I wrote this book. So let's take this journey together. I want to start with my story so continue reading and understand that I've been where you are and I can tell you, the top of the mountain is a beautiful place to live.

3

Doing the work!

Before we get to much further into this book, I want to set you on the path to success. The sooner you begin creating new habits for yourself, the sooner you will begin to see positive changes happening in your life. This book is about helping you figure out exactly what you want for your life. At the end of the next few chapters, I'm going to ask you some questions to help you write down specifically what makes you, uniquely you. You start figuring out what you want out of life (because I know it is not an easy task) by asking the right questions. Here are some questions to help stimulate your thinking. Just be honest, and don't think about how you'll make the changes right now, just write down your answers.

I am happiest when I am:

_____

_____

I like to be around people who are:

_____

_____

I am motivated by:

_____

_____

I'm most interested in:

_____

_____

I love to learn about:

_____

_____

My Story

I can remember the day clearly. It was a sunny, beautiful fall day, with clear skies and I was just waking up. I was tired, uninspired and felt no real sense of passion or purpose. At this time in my life I was a bartender as my line of work. I really enjoyed the work and being around people who I could talk with, laugh with and even help at times.

However, on this particular day I woke up with this feeling of emptiness and unhappiness. Now, my life was a good one. I had a family, a wife, two kids, and a job. I had, what most people would consider a good life. Don't get me wrong, I was thankful for what I had and thankful for the blessings that were in my life. Nonetheless, I still felt this emptiness inside. I laid in bed wondering what was missing from my life. From the outside looking in my life looked like I wanted it to look. I loved being a father, I was doing okay financially, and at that time my life was where I thought it should be. So why was I feeling this emptiness?

I realized that I was viewing my life and creating my life from the outside in. I realized that I wanted to have a family and I wanted to have children and I wanted to have a comfortable life. I had in fact created the exact life I had envisioned for myself. It was at that moment that I realized what I hadn't done. I never created my life from the inside out. I created my life from the idea that if I wanted to have the family and the children and the house and a comfortable life that I would need to do what it took to get those things. I had successfully created the life I thought I should have.

Now, I did what most people do. I went to school, I was employed, and I made good money, I got married and I had children. What I thought I wanted, I had created. So if I had the life that I wanted and I had done what I needed to do to make it happen, why was I still feeling like something was missing? It was that moment in my life that I realized exactly what I had done. I had created my life, I designed it, I did everything I needed to do to make it happen, but I did it in the exact opposite order that I was supposed to do it in. I had created my life from the outside in and I should've been creating it from the inside out.

On the surface I was a happy guy. I was smiling, I was pretty fulfilled, and I looked like I was a guy who had everything a guy could ask for, a guy who was living a good life. On the inside however, there was still a void, a really empty void. I wasn't being who I knew I could be. I wasn't living my life for myself. Of course, I needed to be responsible and provide for my family, that goes without saying. So in many ways I had the responsibility to live my life in a certain way so that I could be responsible for providing for those people that relied on me and I welcomed that responsibility.

I loved providing for my family. I still, to this day love every moment of having a family, it remains my most important job in the world. Being a dad is my favorite job, yet I had forgotten the most important aspect of my life. I had forgotten this was my life.

It wasn't the life that I was living just to support my family. Sure, I had a family and I was a father but I was also me, and I wasn't being uniquely me. I kind of forgot that this was the one chance that I get on this earth to be what I want to be, to create the life I want to create, and then leave it behind for the people that are here when I'm gone.

When I finally realized that, I got disgusted. When I realized that I was living my life just to fill the needs of other people, that really bothered me. Again, don't mistake what I'm saying here for a selfish act or a self-centered way of thinking. I realized that I wasn't living my life by my own choosing based on what I wanted as a core inner drive. If I wasn't doing that than I wasn't really being everything I could be. I wasn't providing everything I could provide for my family and for the people around me, and I certainly wasn't providing it for myself. I now know that in order to provide properly and give everything I had to my family, to the people I love, and those around me I needed to live my life from the inside out. The problem was I had no idea what I wanted for my life! I had no idea what made me uniquely me and what would provide me with that sense of fulfillment that I was longing for. What was it?

So with that new understanding of my life, with that new realization, I began to search for who I wanted to be. I went back to doing what I felt I was good at as a career. You see, I am and always have been a creator, I am a very creative thinker. I went to college as an industrial design major. That was the study of product and idea development and other various forms of creativity and design. When I began my search for who I was, I did what I do best. I began creating new ideas for products that I thought would help the world and what I thought the world really needed.

Like most creative types, as soon as I started to generate new ideas, I was energized! I found a new sense of passion and excitement in

7

my life because I was creating again. I began developing new ideas and for the first time in many years my mind was full of inspired energy. I felt alive again and I was creating products, designing marketing plans, and developing emerging business ideas that I was going to bring to market. I was one hundred percent confident that this was my life's purpose and what I was supposed to be doing. With this newfound energy, I felt alive. I was having meetings with product developers and presenting my ideas to the people that could make them happen. Within just a short amount of time after creating several ideas that I knew would change the world I confidently presented them to the people who I knew could bring them to market. I'm pleased to tell you that as soon as I started to do what made me happy, I did it! I failed!

I didn't bring a single product to market. Still to this day, I have a desk that has drawings in it that really never became anything more than just an idea. I was never someone who lacked for ideas and creativity. I went to design school, not because I was a great artist, but because I was full of ideas and I had an inner creative spirit. So if I had so many 'really good' ideas that could change the world and I could design and create, then why wasn't I having any success?

That's when I had another realization of my life. I realized that I was attempting to create these products for pure financial gain only. I approached my ideas from the question of "What can I create that the world would buy and I would get rich?" Of course, if you're rich you can have all the money to provide the life you've always wanted right? If I had everything I wanted in my life then I would be happy and fulfilled? Nope, wrong again Tom, completely wrong.

I sure was failing a lot. However, as I want you to realize, you need to recognize what isn't working in your life before you can fix it. You need to understand and acknowledge why you're failing before you can succeed. The lessons I learned from those failures and the realizations I had from those failures were some of the most valuable, and expensive, failures I've ever had in my life. Yet in order to truly fail you would have to completely stop right? You would have to just give up and never proceed forward. That's not what I did.

One of my favorite quotes is from Henry David Thoreau. He said, "If one advances confidently in the direction of his dreams and endeavors to live the life which he has imagined, he will meet with a success unexpected in common hours." That quote always reminded me to never give up, and to proceed with confidence in what I envisioned as possible. When you do so, your failures are not failures but simply learning experiences that will provide you with the foundation for your success in the future. I never really looked at my failures as failures. I looked at what didn't work in my life as a way of learning what needed to be improved upon. By viewing my life in this way I wasn't held back for long when I did fall off track because I, much like you, have plenty of times when I have fallen off track. The trick is to get up, clean yourself off, and get back on track and back into momentum quickly so you can continue to advance confidently in the direction of your dreams.

When I began to look at why I had failed to bring my 'life-changing' products to market something became very clear to me. None of the products that I had designed came from within my heart and my spirit. They were all designed from the outside. I was creating these products in an attempt to create an income that I thought would provide me with the fulfillment that I was longing for in my life. After all, I was being creative, which is what I love to be. I was designing, which is what I love to do. I was even designing products that I thought would help improve people's lives. So why wasn't I successful? Because I was focused on the wrong aspect of success. Throughout this course you're going to learn how to create your life from the inside out and yes without a doubt you're going to get anything and everything you want from an external point of view as well, if you do the work.

I needed to share the story of my life with you so that you knew that I've struggled to create the life I wanted, exactly the same way you may have struggled. I've struggled with creating personal success, as well as fulfillment, and it took me many, many years to finally understand the difference between what it takes to truly succeed and how not to fail. I can tell you real quickly how to not fail if that's what you're hoping to get out of this book. I'll tell you right now and you can stop reading. If you don't want to fail than quite simply, don't take action. Don't ever get into momentum, and don't ever consciously create the life of your dreams. I can pretty much guarantee if you just sit on the couch, never actually doing anything to create the life you want, you will most likely never fail. If that was the information you were looking for from this book then this is the point where you can stop reading and return it, this book is not for you. You can go back to living the life you've always lived. Thank you for your time and your interest in creating the life you want and I wish you all the best. However, if you are ready and willing to do what it takes to succeed, keep reading.

Here are some more questions for you to answer about yourself. Keep doing this work, you're doing great!

My ideal work would be:

_____

_____

I am skilled at:

_____

_____

If I could, I would:

_____

_____

To love my life I would have to:

_____

_____

Financially I want to be:

_____

_____

For The Committed People

Now since you're still reading I'm going to take an educated guess that you don't simply want to know how not to fail. You, in fact, want to know how to succeed. Not just how to succeed but how to succeed at the highest level possible. Since you are still reading I want to thank you. I want to thank you for being someone who is committed to creating the life that you want to live and acknowledge your desire to make that happen. You see, there are two types of people in this world. There are people who are interested in creating their life, and then there are the people who are committed to creating their lives and making it everything they've ever wanted. You my friend are committed to creating your life and that is a very rare quality.

So what was the realization I had? What was it that allowed me to take my life from where I was to where I wanted to be? Well, I'll tell you. The difference came when I decided something. Since I realized that I was not creating my life from the inside out, from that moment on I decided to look at what would make me truly happy. From that moment I chose to create my life from the inside out, not from the outside in.

Now please understand, I did not wake up one day, have a moment of clarity, and in the same day write this book and put it out there for the world. It didn't happen that way. There's a long period of about ten years in between when I first started telling you that story and now when I'm writing this book. I don't remember where I heard it but somewhere along the way in my life I heard someone say that it takes about ten years of hard work to become an overnight success. I wish I could remember who told me that because I'd like to thank them for that wisdom which, at the time, I really didn't understand but now that statement is perfectly clear to me.

I'm not here to give you some false hope that when you finish this book that you will somehow magically have the life you've always wanted, I'm not that guy. I'm not that person who is going to fill your head with false hopes of get rich quick and setting up an automated system to your success. Now, I'm not saying that those people can't teach you how to do that, what I'm telling you is that this book isn't even about success from a financial standpoint so to speak. Although the principles and the skills and the tools you'll learn in this book, can in fact, be used to create a life of extreme wealth. I want something more for you. I want you to feel a sense of fulfillment and gratefulness in your life that money can't provide.

If you brought with you to this book, 'I want to get rich,' and that's all that's important to you then this probably isn't the right book for you. I want to show you how to create a life of wealth from the inside out, a life where no matter what you do and don't have, you are completely fulfilled. Once you have that. you can go on and learn how to create financial success. Now don't get me wrong, I want you to be wealthy if you want to be wealthy.

However, I designed this book, in its entirety, from the belief that you want a life of purpose and passion. Once I teach you how to live a life of purpose and passion, with a vision for everything you want in your life, then we can talk about how to get wealthy, using that purpose and using that passion if you want to.

For now, just know this. Before we begin, I want you to bring with you to this book anything you want. Yes, you can bring 'I want to get rich,' that's okay, bring it with you no matter what it is. If you have an internal desire to be happier, or healthier, or more loving, or more compassionate, bring that with you too. Maybe you have an external desire. Is it a brand-new car, a house, a boat, lavish vacations? Whatever you want, I'll show you how to get it, so bring it! Bring what you want to this time we have together and most of all be here while you're reading this book. Be one hundred percent present while you are reading, and participate in the activities provided. We are going to do activities in this book that are going to help you to get your mind right, and then ultimately at the end, you are going to see exactly where your life is going. By the time you finish this book, you're going to know exactly how to get where you want to be in life but if you don't do the work, well then, nothing's going to change.

Do you have something that you want in your life? Are you ready to do the work and do you have the desire to make your life exactly what you want it to be? Do you want to live your life with no excuses while letting nothing and no one hold you back? If you said 'Yes' then we can get started.

Here are a few more questions.

In my relationship I want:

_____

_____

For my health I want to:

_____

_____

I absolutely want

_____

_____

_____ in my life!

Having

_____

_____

_____ matters to me!

I would like to spend more time:

_____

_____

Even if I never made a cent, I would like to work on:

_____

_____

Let's Get It Started!

So this section of the book is called the ABCs of Success. I designed this section as a way of helping you learn how to achieve goals in your life. You may have taken some goal setting courses, or even taken a lot of self-development courses in the past. If that's the case, well then I invite you to really participate in this section anyway. Typically, no matter how much you know there is something within a book that will give you a new perspective on life. If you get one bit of knowledge out of this section of the book that you've never acquired before, well great, that might be the item you need to take your life to 'The Next Level.'

The reason I really wanted to create the ABCs of Success is because if I can teach you and you can learn how to achieve one goal, just one thing in your life that you really want, then you can learn how to create any goal and how to achieve anything you want in your life. My goal for you in the ABCs of Success section is to learn how to achieve a single goal. However, my vision for you, at the end of the entire book is to show you a literal roadmap of how you can create the life you want, no matter what it is.

There's a place where you are right now and a place where you want to be. I'm going to show you how to get where you want to be. No traditional education anywhere in the world does that. Sure there are courses you can take, but kids don't go to school to learn how to create their lives and most adults don't go to school to learn how to design their lives. Even most colleges don't teach you how to identify your purpose and your passion in life.

I'm going to ask that you don't be most people. Most people just go to school, hopefully get a good job, and maybe years and years later they might even retire. That's sort of the path everyone's following. There's a leader or someone who says 'follow me,' I can show you how to live a good life and how to hopefully retire someday so you can spend a few years doing what you want to do. Retire? Aren't people already tired of what they're doing? Being tired all over again doesn't sound like much fun to me as far as a life.

How about doing exactly what you want to do your entire life, working on exactly what it is you want to work on, and re-awakening in your life again! Most people give up on their goals at a pretty early point in their life. Now, call it getting older, responsibility, life gets in the way or whatever other excuse you may have used. However, when did life become just about earning money from something in order to make that work worthwhile? The reality of igniting the passion of life is when you find your purpose, you do it whether you make money or not. Yes, ideally you can turn your passion into a career. Nonetheless, would you sacrifice a daily life of happiness just because you weren't being paid for doing what makes you truly happy? Most people do, it's an unfortunate way of life.

I don't want that for you. I want you to live an amazing life. I want you to know, anything you want for your life is possible.

Living the life you want is more possible today than it's ever been, ever in the history of the world. We have the technology today and books like this one which can teach you how to live any style of life you want. So don't be most people, don't give up on your goals, don't give up on your dreams and what you thought was possible when you were a kid. Don't give up on your happiness just because you haven't yet found a way to earn an income from it. I did that for many years, and I found myself in a place of loneliness, boredom, and frustration, because I was distant from my Maker's true purpose for my life.

When somebody asked you what you wanted to be, as a kid, I bet you didn't say, "I want to be employed in a job I don't like." That's not what kids say! They give you an answer based on what they believe will make them happy in life. So here's what I'm going to ask you to do. I'm going to ask you to trust me. Trust me and trust this process. What is the very worst thing that can happen if you read this entire book and you spend some of your time learning what I'm going to teach you? The worst thing that can happen is nothing changes.

You'll still have enough to eat, I hope. You'll still have shelter, I hope. You'll still have access to water, I hope. You'll still be able to sleep, I hope. You see, those are the basic needs you require in your life. Now, I hope you have all of those necessities right now, but I'm not here to provide you with what you need. I'm here to provide you with the knowledge of how to get what you want. So trust me and trust this process, because the best thing that can happen is, you do this work, you take the information you read, you put it into action, and you create the exact life you want to live!

Your life probably won't take a drastic turn after you finish this book. Life may not even be that different the next day, maybe not the week, the month, or year after this one, but at some point I want you to live the life you want to live. Are you going to say you are living your ideal life, doing what you're doing right now? I'd have to guess that the answer is no. Is everything you could envision for yourself possible by doing what you're doing right now, based on the way you are designing your life? Answer that question honestly, if the answer is no, then you should get excited! This book is going to teach you what you need to know in order to create the life you may only be dreaming about right now!

So participate. Do what I'm going to ask you to do in this book. Use it, use this information, use my time, use my passion, and my enthusiasm for doing what I do, which is to help you... Wake up!! You have a life to live. Each and every day should be filled with passion and purpose. Did you forget that somewhere along the way? I know I did!

Now listen, you might mess up, you might fail, you might fall completely flat on your face, maybe even get bloody or break a bone. I hope not, I hope with everything I have, none of those things happen to you. I can pretty much guarantee if you are going to just sit on the couch and do nothing then you probably won't fail. I want you to understand something though, you might mess up. When you're creating your life, you might make things worse before they get better. You're learning! Your entire life, when you learned how to do something, you messed up in the beginning, you didn't do it perfectly, so mess up but don't give up. Your life is your journey. Enjoy the process. Enjoy the journey. Don't spend so much time focused on where you want to be that you forget that you're here right now learning how to design your life. This is your life! Wake up and live in this moment!

Fill in the blank

"I will allow myself to m_____ u___,

but I will not allow myself to g____ u___!"

Don't reinvent the wheel!

Now, you could go out right now and for the next ten years do what I did. You could read book after book on success, you could watch hours and hours of video, take personal development courses, listen to audios, go to live seminars. You can spend the next ten years doing what I've spent the last ten years doing. But why would you do that? I've done that for you. I've done that work. Learn from my mistakes. Learn from my successes.

I've taken everything that I've learned about success, and failure, and mindset and goal setting, and psychology, and creating the life you want and I've boiled it down. I've extracted all unneeded stuff and I put what you do need into this book. This section specifically, the ABCs of Success, are the fundamentals of the game of life. Ask any coach and they'll tell you that you have to be great at the fundamentals if you're going to be the top player. Be better than others at doing what it takes to win the game and you will win.

I want to show you how to design a Ferrari of a car. I want you to design a life beyond what you can see possible right now. I want people to laugh at you, I want them to say "that's not possible." However, just like that car, you can design a Ferrari of a life. If it doesn't have wheels, a fundamental element of its design, then you're not going to go anywhere. That car is useless. Now I could, right now, show you how to create, and design, and live the exact life you want, but if you don't know the fundamentals then you're not going to get anywhere.

You see, people who are confused about life don't do anything with their life. So my goal is to take the confusion out of life. I want to take you step by step through what it takes to achieve the simplest of goals and then we're going to move up and we're going to learn what it takes to achieve bigger goals. Then we are going to move up even farther and eventually we are going to get to the point where you can envision a life for yourself that you've never even dreamed in your wildest imagination was possible. I'm not going to just stop and let you keep dreaming. I'm going to give you the tools and the knowledge and inspiration and everything you need to take the life that you'll envision and go out and live it! Isn't that what you want?

No matter what you want, you need to live your life with purpose and passion and enthusiasm and energy. It's not hard to live that life. I have the skills, I have the knowledge, I have the ability to show you how to do that, but what I don't have is the ability to make you do it. You have to create *your* life. I can show you exactly how but I can't take the steps for you.

What I am telling you is that if you just read this information and don't ever put it into action in your life then nothing will change. Your knowledge will increase, your ability to create your life will improve, your thoughts will change. But your actual life will not. See the key to having a great life is having a progressive series of great years. The key to having a successive series of great years is to have a series of great months. The key to having a great month is to have a series of great days. The key to having a great day is to learn how to make each moment count.

Well, that's what this book is all about. This book is about making the moments of your life count. Those moments matter! Because those moments add up to seconds, which add up to minutes, then to hours, and to days, weeks and months. That time adds up to the years in your life and what you have is a series of moments that pass by. If you don't live in these moments, you'll look back years from now and you'll say, "Wow, I sure missed out on a lot of really great moments in my life."

Moment by moment, day by day is all we have, that makes up our lives. In those moments we create our lives. Goal by goal, achievement by achievement, by doing what needs to be done. That's how you create your life. This book is going to help you to become more aware of this fact. I don't want you any longer to allow time to pass you by. Time is your most precious resource, don't squander it! Do you doubt that time is your most precious resource? Do you not agree? You might say "time, I don't want time, I want money!"

Let me ask you something. If you were to ask anybody who's no longer with us, anyone that's passed away, what do you think they would rather have, one more day on earth or all the money in the world? I guarantee, if you were to ask anybody who has died if they would choose one more day on earth or all the money in the world, they would give up everything they ever had financially. They wouldn't give one consideration to money. They would take the 24 hours they had and they would use their time wisely. They would use every single moment they had, to create the life they wanted even for that one day.

One final question for you.

If this year were my last year on earth, and I knew it, I would:

_____

_____

_____

What Are You Going To Learn

So what are you really going to learn in the ABCs of Success? I want to give you an overview of this section, so you'll know what to expect from this part of the book. Again, these are the fundamentals, these are the basics, these are so basic I'm calling them the ABCs of Success. How much more basic can you get? The ABCs of Success are so simple, literally a child can learn them the same way they learn the ABCs song. Ideally, once you learn the ABCs of Success they'll be running over in your head all day long and you'll say, "okay, just do the ABCs of Success! I know what I want, what do I need to do to get it?" The first thing we're going to do is cover this deceptively simple lesson.

The next thing we're going to cover is mindset. How are you thinking? What kind of mindset do you have? You need to have a certain type of mindset to achieve what you want to achieve. If you don't believe something is possible well then, you're not going to ever do it. You're going to say, "That's not even possible so why should I even bother taking action."

After mindset you're going to learn about goal setting. More importantly you're going to learn about goal achieving. You see, I don't want you to just set goals in your life that you never achieve; I want you to put the smack down on your goals. That's what I'm going to teach you how to do, put the smack down on your goals. You're going to say, "No more letting my goals go unachieved!" I'm not going to allow you to just create something that you want in your life. Yes, I want you to be a goal setting genius. But there are a lot of geniuses in this world who aren't living the life they want. So I want you to be a goal achieving genius.

After you learn the fundamentals of goal setting and how to put the smack down on your goals, you're going to learn about time management. How are you going to find the time to do what you've always wanted to do but you haven't had the time to do it? How am I possibly going to teach you how to find time? Now listen, I understand, I'm a busy guy. I have five kids and those kids keep me busy! Trust me, I understand we are busy in our lives, but that doesn't give you the right to not live the life you want. It's your life, it's not just your kid's life. You are in your kid's lives and they are in your life but they are not your entire life. Yes, I want them to be an integral part of your life. Put everything you have into being the best parent you can be, if you have kids. If you don't have kids, well all the more power to you, you have more 'available' time. You might be very, very busy, I'm not taking that away from you. No matter what your situation is, I'm never going to allow you to use time as an excuse ever again.

After time management we're going to talk about your associations. Your associations are who and what you associate with in your life and how those associations are affecting your ability to create the life you want, and more importantly, just how those associations are stopping you from achieving, sometimes, the simplest goals in your life.

Right after associations, we're going to talk about energy. What are you doing in your life right now that's draining your energy? We're going to identify those things and then we're also going to identified how you can produce energy. You need to have energy if you're going to achieve your goals. So if you're doing everything in your life to reduce your energy, are you going to have what it takes to achieve your goals? You're not. So we're going to teach you how to generate energy.

Then we're going to talk about what to expect. What do you need to expect of yourself and what are you going to need to expect of other people when you are creating your life and working to achieve your goals? You need to have expectations, but you need to have the right kind of expectations.

Following that section, you'll learn how to put yourself first. It is not selfish to put yourself first when you create your life. When you take time for yourself, you make everything around you better. You make the lives of the people around you better by putting yourself first. So stop putting yourself off, stop making you insignificant. You matter, what you do matters. So I'm going to teach you how to put yourself first.

When you learn how to put yourself first, then we're going to talk about your intuition. We'll talk about those times when you say, "I should have done that," or, "oh man, I shouldn't have done that." You're going to learn how to recognize when you should immediately take action and when you should step back and say, no, it's not the right time.

Once you understand all the things we are going to talk about in the ABCs of Success we're going to put it into action because, again, this book is not about wanting what it is you desire in your life, this course is about doing what it takes to get it.

To begin, like I said, we're going to start simple. In fact, I want to keep this information simple. I have found, and I believe, if life is complicated then you're not doing it right. I like to keep things really simple. I've always had a good skill for taking what's seemingly complicated and breaking it down into a simplistic form other people can understand. We're going to start in the simplest way I could conceive. We are going to start with the ABCs of Success.

Before we do, I want to say congratulations. I want to congratulate you for taking action in your life. By reading this book you are taking action. You might not realize it, you might just say, "I bought this book and I hope it's going to change my life." But that's taking action, and that is the first critical element of your success. So acknowledge yourself for the fact that you are taking action. You've gotten this far in the book; you haven't gotten sick of me yet. You're doing something to create your life, so congratulations for that accomplishment. Acknowledge yourself for every accomplishment. Give yourself credit.

That's the difference between people who achieve what they want in their life and those that don't. There are two different types of people. There are talkers and there are doers. Many people just simply talk about what they want in their life. Many people say "I want this in my life, I want that in my life," but they don't actually do anything to make it happen. They talk about it all the time. You don't see them for a year and you say, "how's it going" and they talk about the same thing. They might have added a few more items to their "to do" list but they aren't actually doing anything. They're not changing their lives, they're not taking action, and they're not being a doer. I'm going to ask you from this point on in your life, if you have been a talker, to be a doer.

Make the choice. Choose to be in action. Choose to do the things it takes to create your life. No more excuses. Taking action is the absolute first key to your success. Change in life happens at the level of action. If you don't ever spark the match can you create fire? Yes, I get it, you can rub sticks together, but you're still taking action when you're rubbing the sticks together. If there's no spark, there's no fire. So what you need is that spark. If you have that spark within you right now, even if you didn't have it before, and right now you have it, that's what I need from you. That spark is what you need to create the A in the ABCs of Success.

The ABCs of Success

You must take action. You must take action on what you want in your life. Now here are some examples. A lot of people say, I want to lose weight but they don't actually take any action to lose weight. Some people say, I want to make more money, but they don't ever take any action to make more money. Other people say, I want to be a better parent, but they don't ever take any action to be a better parent. You can want everything in your life but unless you do what it takes you're not going to have it.

So if you want to lose weight you have to plan an exercise routine. You have to plan a nutrition routine. You have to plan. But don't get stuck in planning mode. Plan what you're going to do and then take action. If your goal is to earn more money, you have to choose what you are going to do to earn more money and then you have to go out and you have to do it. No matter what you want to do, planning is a major key to your success and planning is the start of taking action. Planning is an action. But a lot of people get stuck in what's known as analysis paralysis. They analyze what they have to do to make their life what they want, and they just think about it. They don't actually do anything.

Yes, planning is a very important first action but actually doing what you plan on doing is much more important. I'm going to say if you don't have a plan but you take action, it's better than if you have a plan but don't take action. Now of course you've probably heard before if you fail to have a plan, you're planning to fail. But if you have a plan and you don't take action, the plan isn't going to do you any good. It's going to sit on the table and you're going to get a coffee spill on it and then you're going to throw it away. You're going to go back to living your life the way it was. So I say plan, but more importantly take action. So do you have it? Do you understand the most critical element; I'm going to drill it into your head. What is the A in the ABCs of Success? Action! They yell it when they do anything in Hollywood, action! Take action!

Since this is the ABCs of Success, the next element you need to learn is the B. The B in the ABCs of Success is belief. Belief is the foundation; belief is everything you build upon. If you take action but you don't believe it's possible, you'll be building on a weak foundation and likely crumble. Everything you do is built upon the foundation of belief. If you believe that you can lose weight and you believe you can lose weight easily, you're going to take the actions necessary to lose that weight. You're going to make the right choices. You're going to say, "No, I don't want that, I want this" when faced with a food choice. You're going to do the exercising you need to do. You're going to eat right. You're going to have the mindset of someone who successfully loses weight.

Your brain is a very, very powerful tool in getting what you want. If you believe you can earn a certain amount of money, that is what you'll have the ability to earn. Sporadically you might earn a little bit more but consistently you will not earn the type of money you want to earn unless you believe earning that amount of money is possible. You've got to believe it. Your belief is what you allow into your life. What you believe, you can achieve. You need to make a positive belief foundation the core of who you are.

Say, "I believe….." what? What you'll likely see is your life lining up with that belief. This works both positively and negatively. You take actions, upon your beliefs. We're going to cover much more about this throughout this book. For now, believe me, because I'm going to prove to you, your life is literally built upon your belief system.

Now the difference is, you've got to believe what you want is what you're going to be committed to achieving. See, for me I believe this is my purpose in life. I believe I have the ability to positively influence people's lives all around the world so they can go out and they can find their purpose and their passion and they can create the life they want. I want to believe that is true, so I take the actions necessary to live that belief and I'm one hundred percent committed to this belief.

There are people who are committed to doing what they say they are going to do because it's what they believe in. It's what they create their life to be. Then there are people who are just interested. People who say, "That sounds good, maybe I'll do that some day." Those people are interested, the other people are committed. I'm not interested in changing people's lives, I'm not interested in changing your life, I'm committed to changing your life and I'll do whatever I have to do to make that possible. I'll do everything in my power to help you to create and live the exact life you want to live. I am committed to it because I'm being that in my life. I am doing what it takes to have the ability to see that manifested in our lives, and to have the pleasure of seeing you create and live the life you want to live.

We're going to talk about this in great detail but I want you to remember this pattern. If you want to have something in your life you don't have it first and then do what's necessary to keep it, in order to be what it is you want to be. You don't have the luxury house and lifestyle, do what you need to do to keep it, and then be who you need to be in order to keep it. The pattern of success is be, do, and have. You have to *be* first. You have to *be*lieve it. You have to *be*come it to *be* who you want to *be* in your life. Then you have to *do* what you have to *do*. You have to take action.

Some people might say you have to believe it even before you take action. That's true to a certain extent. Yes, you have to believe it, you have to be it, you have to see it in your mind, and to make it real for yourself. But belief can only get you so far. Belief won't get you off the couch. Action will get you off the couch. Belief keeps you in your head. Action gets you into life. Sometimes, taking the action, helps you to build the belief system, and sometimes the belief system helps you take action.

One is not more important than the other, both are critically important elements of your success, these are the A B C's of Success. If you want to be what you want to be in your life, believe it, become it, then do what you need to do. Take the actions to *have* what you want in your life then you can have it. So that's the pattern of success. The ABCs are the critical elements, *be, do, have* is the pattern.

You've probably heard me mention commitment during the ABCs of Success, so if you guessed the C in the ABCs of Success is commitment, then you're wrong! Because the C is not commitment, that's important, you have to be committed but that's not the C in the ABCs of Success. The C in the ABCs of Success is consistency. If you're committed to what you want to be and what you want to do then you're going to be consistent. If you're just interested in what you want in your life then you're going to lack consistency. You can still achieve success if you're not consistent, but if you are consistent your success will come so much faster. So put it into action, believe it's possible, and be consistent. Those are the ABCs of Success.

Here are some examples of consistency. Can a fireman who wants to build a great cavern in a mountain do so by blasting a solid rock with a fire hose for a week straight, staying up with every bit of energy he has, holding the hose blasting it at full power. Can he create that same cavern, consistently flowing water will form over time? No. He would get too tired, and eventually burn out or give up.

Most people, year after year, talk about achieving the same goals. I've done it myself; I'm not saying that I'm innocent with this challenge. I've just learned how to think differently and how to be more consistent. In fact, consistency is what I struggle with the most. It's without a doubt, the most difficult element of success.

Most people year after year start the same goals. What do people say, "I want to lose weight, I want to make more money." New Year's Day, people declare, "I'm starting my goals!!" February 1ˢᵗ, what happened to those goals, their gone right? Well there's always next year.

That's what people do, year after year. There's no consistency. I want you to practice staying consistent. Just complete one goal after the other even if they're small. Stay in momentum, be consistent, and don't stop in your race. I know you've heard about the tortoise and the hare, isn't it consistency that allows the tortoise to win the race? That hare is starting and stopping, taking a nap, starting and stopping, taking a nap. The hare's exhausted, expending a lot of energy in the beginning. Giving it everything he's got and then he stops. That's what most people do, don't be most people! Take action, believe in yourself, and be consistent.

Let me give some examples of how consistency can make a massive difference in your life. Let's just say that you want to get in shape. I understand you just don't have time to go to the gym and we're going to deal with time issues. Maybe you don't. Maybe you are so busy you just don't have the time. I can't magically create time, although I am going to show you later in this book, at a minimum, how to create six days of time this year, and no it's not a magic trick. I'm not going to tell you something's possible and then not show you how to do it. I'm going to show you how to create six literal days of time in your life this year. Time that is completely yours, to use for whatever you want. I'll show you how to create 30 days of time if you need that, but here's what I want to show you about consistency.

Let's just say that you want to lose some weight, you want to start exercising, but you just can't seem to get to the gym. What if you just said "I'm going to do thirty push-ups every single day." Could you hit the floor right now and do thirty push-ups in a row? It's not that easy. You have to be in pretty good shape to do thirty push-ups in a row. Is it possible you could do ten push-ups even if you had to do them on your knees because you're getting started? Even if they aren't perfect, we're not talking about perfect here, we're talking about taking action. Let's just say you're going to do ten push-ups but you're going to do that three times a day. Maybe before you have breakfast you're going to do ten push-ups. Before you have lunch you're going to do ten push-ups. Before you have dinner you're going to do ten more push-ups. You're going to get your energy flowing and that will help you burn off more calories while increasing your metabolism.

So with your goal of losing weight you're going to help yourself by doing little things to help you achieve that goal. So you decide that you're going to do thirty push-ups every single day this year. I'm not saying it's easy but it is simple. If you were to do ten push-ups, three times per day, three hundred and sixty five days this year. You will do ten thousand nine hundred and fifty push-ups this year! Now, if you don't do any push-ups right now do you think that will make a difference in how you feel, and look, and in your strength? You better believe it will and how long does it take you to do ten push-ups? Twenty seconds? Are you telling me that you can't find one minute, twenty seconds in the morning, twenty seconds in the afternoon, and twenty seconds in the evening to do ten push-ups at a time? One minute out of the twenty four hours you have in your day to do ten thousand nine hundred and fifty push-ups this year? Come on now, you're just making excuses.

How about increasing your knowledge? Most people don't read any books after they leave school. So let's just say again, you are going to read five pages in the morning, five pages in the afternoon, and five pages at night. Could you read five pages when you wake up in the morning? I know you're busy, but isn't it possible to read five pages when you wake up in the morning, you jump into your book to wake up your mind. How about in the afternoon, you take your lunch break, take your book with you, and read five more pages. It doesn't have to be at the same time but read five pages in the afternoon. In the evening before you go to bed instead of watching television, read something to help your mind calm down from the day. If you read five pages three times a day, you read fifteen pages a day. If you're going to do that every single day and you do that for a two weeks you read two hundred and ten pages in two weeks.

There are a lot of success books out there, and they aren't even all as long as this one. There are tons of topic specific books that teach you exactly what it is that you need to learn to be able to do what you need to do to create the life you want to live. So if you read two hundred and ten pages, every other week, you're reading 2 books a month. If you read 2 books per month, you're reading twenty six books this year! Twenty six books, are you kidding me, most people don't read more than three books for their entire adult life. Do you know how many pages that is in a year? That's over five thousand pages of knowledge that would be going into your head and helping you to create the life you want to create! Now do you see how consistency is really, really powerful?

The success equation is action, plus belief, plus consistency, equals success. So what do you want to do? What do you want to do more consistently this year that will move you forward towards achieving the life you want to live? Just choose a simple goal you haven't done yet. Put it into the success equation. What do you need to believe about achieving that goal? What action are you going to take, and how consistently are you going to do it? Perform the equation and that'll equal your success. Remember the success equation; action, plus belief, plus consistency, equals success.

Mindset

I told you after we learned the ABCs of Success, which I hope you understand now, we were going to talk about your mindset. We talked a little bit about belief. Belief is a vital element to your success. So what's the difference between beliefs and mindset? Your mindset is your beliefs. Your mindset is what you believe can happen. Your mindset is your foundation of your beliefs.

Think of your mindset as the concrete upon which houses, skyscrapers, and suspension bridges are built. You must build on the rock. Despite what you may think right now, you are not born with your beliefs and your mindset. You accept, and then solidify your beliefs over your lifetime. Just like concrete accepts water, and then solidifies. The good news is, just like concrete, your beliefs, mindset, and thoughts can be shattered, and then reformed so that you can begin again. Even a small crack in an otherwise strong foundation can compromise the structure which is built upon the foundation. So too, if a small crack in your foundational belief system is worked on over time, it can compromise the integrity of your mindset.

Your beliefs, and therefore your mindset are the literal foundation for everything you do in life. I'm going to draw this out for you later on in this book, and you'll see that what I'm saying is one hundred percent true. If you don't believe you can build something you'll never get it off the ground. So your beliefs and your mindset, are quite simply solidified by your thoughts. Just like everything changes with action, everything starts with your thoughts.

I want to introduce you to a bad word, a four-letter word. I don't want you to use this word improperly. Sure there are times when you can use this word appropriately, but do not use this four letter word improperly or it can sabotage everything in your life. The word I'm talking about is can't, C-A-N-T. You can't use can't improperly if you want to achieve your goals. What does can't stand for? The C in c.a.n.t. stands for can't.

How many times do you hear people say it? "I can't do that, I tried but I can't do it. I can't find the time. I can't find the money. I just can't find the desire. I can't find the willpower. I can't seem to get myself motivated." Have you ever heard people say that before? Can't is an awful, awful word so I'm telling you right now you can't use the word can't anymore!

Now I understand there are times when people might say "I can't get up" and they have a physical reason, like a broken leg, that keeps them down and obviously they can't get up. That's not the can't I am talking about. The can't I'm talking about is the disempowering belief that you can't do something, based on a belief.. It's a thought, that's all it is. The word can't when you apply it to what you want in your life is incredibly disempowering. It's a thought that disempowers you.

Now the A in c.a.n.t. is always. Always is something that people might use negatively when they say things like, "I always mess that up. I always get to a certain point and I stop losing weight. Every time I go to do that, something always happens to get in my way." Have you ever done this? Have you ever said "I can't do that because this always happens?" Well, now do you see how the C and the A in can't are two really disempowering words?

What about N? Do you use the word never? "I can't do it because this always happens and that never happens. I can never find the time. I never have any energy. I never have any money. I never lose weight. They never do that for me." Never, never, never. It's another horrible word. Can't, always, never. They are three horrible, horrible words that people use all the time, and what are they? They are your thoughts, that's all they are, they are only a thought that you put into words and when you put those thoughts into words you make them real. You put that into your belief system and it begins to solidify like a concrete foundation.

What about the T? "I'm trying to quit smoking. I'm trying to lose weight. I'm trying to start this business so I can make some more money. I'm trying to save enough money so we can buy that new car." Trying? Are you serious, you're trying to do something? What is trying? Trying is not committing. Trying means that you're interested. If you say you are trying to build a business, you are interested in building a business. If you say you are trying to quit smoking, you're interested in quitting smoking. If you're trying to lose weight, you're interested in it. But you're not committed to it. You're trying. So if you mess up, if you fail, if you give up and stop completely, that's okay, you were just trying, right? You never actually said you were going to do it, you just said you were trying.

Do you see how those four words: can't, always, never, and try, start out as thoughts in your head and then they become real because you say them, you declare them and you bring them into existence. When you use those words you solidify your foundational belief system. You say "I can't do this, I always do that, I never do this, I'm trying to do that!" It doesn't get done because you are not committed. You've got to be committed, and that all starts with your mindset. Please don't say that horrible four letter word, especially in front of kids!

Now that you understand the word can't, I'm going to introduce you to two really enormous words. These are enormously powerful words. These are probably the most powerful words in the English language. If you learn how to say them and how to use these words properly in your everyday vocabulary you will become committed. You'll begin to create your life. You will begin to do the things that you need to do because your thoughts, based on these two words, will solidify a belief system of confidence within you.

Get a pen and a piece of paper because you're going to have to write these down in order to really get it. These are huge words and I'll teach you how to spell them. Okay, do you have a pen? The first word is I, just the letter I. The second word is AM.

They're huge and they are the biggest words that you can use in your life. "I am!" I am what? Whatever you say "I am" and follow it with, you will become. "I am smoke free! I am losing weight! I am starting a business! I am doing whatever it takes to create the life I want and live that life in this moment! I am creating it! I am envisioning it! I am doing what I need to do to make it happen! I am believing it's possible! I am consistent! I am living the life I want!" Now how about that for a couple of empowering words!

Whatever you follow 'I am' with you will become. Watch how powerful this can be if you use those two little words, followed by a negative statement. "I am unable to do it. I am a failure. I am a loser. I am going to try this but I don't think I can do it." Are you kidding me, don't do that! Use 'I am' in the positive reference. The same way you use the C-A-N-T words. Say things like "I can't stop because I need to do that. I can't give up, it's what I want for my life and I can't stop doing that right now. I always move forward. I always achieve my goals. I always know exactly what I need to do in the moment. I never give up. I never stop. I will never give up my goals and dreams. I will never stop creating the life I want to live."

Now since most people don't know this, how do you use the word try? Most people don't understand that trying is not possible. Trying doesn't exist, there is no such thing as trying to do anything. You either are or you are not. But since most people don't know that, how can you positively use the word try with other people? You are not going to use the word try anymore because you know that trying is not an empowering word. Even though the word trying is a disempowering word it can be used to gently motivate someone. You can say "Listen, just give it a try." Sometimes saying, "Just do it," is too much for people. So you can say, "Just give it a try, go for it, do your best." That will motivate people and it might even motivate you.

I'm not saying you shouldn't *try* something, what I'm saying is, if you're trying, you're doing. If you give something a try you are taking action. You are doing it. You're not just trying it, you're doing it. You might not succeed. I am not telling you when you do something you're always going to succeed. You might mess up, you might fail, it might take you a really long time to accomplish that goal, but you're not trying, you're doing. When you're doing something and you're not successful it just means that you're doing it, but you haven't achieved it, yet. So that's the difference in mindset. Your mindset is your thoughts and your mindset is your belief. So don't use the words can't, always, never, and try or the words I am in a negative context any longer. But use all of them in the positive, optimistic, outgoing, influential way that those words should be used.

Now how do you begin to create your mindset? How do you begin to create your thoughts the way that you need them to be in order to create the life that you want to have? Well, that's done through affirmations. That's done through repetitive training. It's like building muscle memory. The greatest athletes develop muscle memory by repetitively performing the same action, over and over and over again.

Developing a success mindset is done through writing down specific thoughts, that you want to have, and reading those thoughts and turning them into what you believe. I am going to teach you something you may or may not know. Your brain does not know the difference between what's real and what you tell it. So if you tell your brain "I can't lose weight," then your brain believes that statement. If you tell your brain "I lose weight easily," then your brain believes that statement. If you tell your brain, "I am only able to earn a certain amount of money," well then, that's what your brain allows you to earn on a consistent basis. If you tell your brain," I can earn unlimited amounts of money," that's what your brain believes. Your brain doesn't know the difference. So the question is simple, what do you want to believe?

Along with affirmations, journaling, or simply writing for the sake of getting thoughts out of your head, is a great way to build your mindset. Journaling is a powerful way to bring thoughts into existence. When you get your thoughts onto paper, or even a computer screen, you make them work to your advantage. Especially as you begin to recognize some limiting beliefs which may come out, and show up on your pages. Maybe you use it as a way of keeping notes for yourself, it is up to you how you journal, but journaling is a very powerful way for you to look back and say, "Wow, I am surprised how my thoughts have evolved." Or you could use your journal to repetitively write down what it is that you want to believe. You can use the journal in any way that you want, it's your tool. It also doesn't have to be fancy. A simple notebook, or computer document, can work as a journal.

I'm going to end this section on mindset with a request. I want to ask you to be optimistic in your thoughts and words from now on. If you find yourself thinking a disempowering thought, stop. Reword the statement in a positive way and you'll begin to create a new habit of being optimistic. Science and the study of how our brains work has evolved so much in recent years. There is so much proof that speaking positively, thinking positively, and being an optimist helps you to achieve so much more in your life. It also helps you to feel healthier and be healthier. It boosts your ability to accomplish tasks. It improves your relationships. It helps you in your job. It helps you with your kids. It helps you with your spouse. Being positive is a vitally important element of success in every area of your life. So write down affirmations and use your journal often, daily is best. Whatever you write down, make it positive. Remember, what you tell your brain, and what you consistently feed into your brain, is what it will believe. So tell your brain what you want it to believe.

Below, you'll have the opportunity to create some "I am" statements of your own. Don't skip over these worksheet pages. Remember, do the work!

I am

_____

I am

_____

I am

_____

I am

_____

I am

_____

I am

_____

I am

_____

I am

_____

Goal Achieving

What are your goals? Your goals are something that you want to be, do, or have in your life. They can be anything. You might want to be more loving. You might want to be more fulfilled. You might want to be happier. You might want to be wealthier, you might want to be a better parent, and you might want to be a better spouse. You might want to be a better employee, a better teacher, a better student or anything else. Whatever you want to be, that's a goal. Goals can also be something that you want to do. You might want to go on vacation, you might want to climb Mount Everest, you might want to surf in Hawaii, whatever you want to do, that is also a goal. Whatever you want to have, that too is a goal. Maybe you want to have a new car. Maybe you want to have a new house. Maybe you want to marry the person of your dreams. Maybe you want to have a better body. Whatever you want to be, do, or have is a goal.

Now I'm very tempted sometimes, when I see people who are just wasting their time in life, to go over to them and say WAKE UP!!

I want to smack them; not literally, I'm not a violent person. What I'm talking about is the fact that I do want to say wake-up. People are just sleeping and sleep walking through life, letting life and their moments pass them by. In order to, years from now, not look back and say, "Oh my gosh, I wasted so much time." You're going to need to put the smack down on your goals. Are you ready to do that; are you ready to put the smack down on your goals?

I'm not talking about just saying you are going to do it, I am talking about actually doing it. Saying, "That's it, no more, I'm not going to allow myself to just want that in my life anymore, I'm going to get it!" Again, most people just talk about what they want but they never actually do what it takes to get it. Creating goals and achieving goals is really simple. It's not always easy, but it's really simple and it's incredibly effective when you do it correctly.

You see, goals don't happen subconsciously. Goals don't get accomplished by just thinking about them. You need to be bringing your goals into existence. There is scientific evidence behind all of this and there are things that happen within your brain when you bring your goals into existence. I'm not going to go into that because I don't believe that people need that information in order to know how to achieve their goals. I want you to know exactly how to put the wheels on that Ferrari of a life, but I don't think you personally need to know how to assemble the engine on the vehicle you are going to build. I don't want you to have all the knowledge of how to build the most perfect car in the world and then not know how to put the wheels on. It doesn't make any sense.

So when you put the smack down on your goals, you're going to do it in this way. You're going to really be specific. You're going to be motivated. You're going to be achieving. You're going to be committed and you are going to keep going… KEEP GOING! No matter what your goals are, put the smack down, say, NO MORE QUITTING! Be specific. Be motivated. Be achieving every day. Be committed and keep going. Now, if you haven't put two and two together, obviously, Specific, Motivating, Achieving, Committed, and Keep going, are the first letters that spell SMACK, so yes, I'm talking smack to you. I hope you enjoy some smack talking because that's what we are going to do now. Let's talk S.M.A.C.K.

Creating your goals consciously by writing them down allows two things to happen. First, your mind immediately begins to calculate what it needs to do in order to make that goal happen. Your brain is really powerful in that way. The second thing that happens is the universe begins to align what it needs to align in order for you to have what you want in your life. The first part happens in your brain very quickly. When you're specific about what you want, your brain says, "Okay, I know exactly what I need to do," it calculates it, down to the very last detail. The more specific you are the more power your brain uses to make that goal a reality. That happens instantaneously. As soon as you say, "That's what I want" your brain says, "Okay, I'm awake, I'm ready to make it happen, let's do it." and you get excited about that. You say, "Yeah, that's what I want," and then your brain says, "When are you going to do it" and you say "I don't know!"

You can't do that! You have to be specific. You have to know what you want and also how you're going to get it. You have to write it down. When you write your goal down, two things happen; your brain says, "Okay, got it, calculating and figuring out how to make it happen." The second thing that happens is the universe says, "Ooh, look at this, somebody woke up, somebody knows exactly what they want for their life. I like that kind of person. I like people who know what they want; I'm going to help him get it." However, the universe is a much bigger space than your brain so the universe has a lot more to align.

People often forget something very important, and this is the problem I have with the traditional law of attraction type of thinking. When people learn the typically taught law of attraction, many times people put so much emphasis on the belief that they forget that you have to take action and you have to give enough time for the universe to align what has to happen. Think about all the things that would have to align in order for the universe to create the situations that it wants to create for you to make your plan a reality. Think about all the people, all the things, all the situations and everything that has to occur simultaneously. The universe is working on that all at the same time and you're moving forward as you're creating your goals. As you are taking steps and you're making things happen, at the same time the universe is saying, "alright, he's still going, he's making it happen, I'm lining it all up and we have everything in sync, we know exactly what's going to collide at the same time." Nevertheless, it takes time for the universe to do its job and it can only do that if you are perfectly clear in what you want. You have to be specific.

Now what do I mean by that? Some examples of being specific would be saying, "I'm going to lose twenty pounds in 6 months." Not being specific is when somebody says, "I want to lose weight." Being specific is saying, "I will earn five thousand dollars every single month and I will do that consistently by this date next year." It's not, "I want to make more money." Being specific is saying, "In order to grow my business I will make ten networking calls every day for a month." It's not, "I want to grow my business." Do you see the difference? There's generalizing and there's specific. In order for you to start putting the smack down on your goals you need to be specific.

If you're not specific you don't give your brain and the universe an exact point where they need to end up. You don't have a specific arrival point. Your brain and the universe need that in order to get you what you want. Your brain and the universe want you to have your ideal life, but if you're not specific they get confused and what do confused people and things do? Nothing! So be specific. What *exactly* do you want?

You can use your journal as a place to write down your goals. Write down your specific goal, and then write down some steps you are going to take to achieve that goal. Again, you need to be specific in the steps you're going to take. What's the first step in losing twenty pounds? The first step is losing 1 pound so make that a step. The next step is also losing 1 pound. If you continue those same 1 pound steps 10 times you have lost 10 pounds. Then continue the steps until you have the number of pounds that you want to lose, in this case, twenty pounds. Each time you lose a pound you can mark it as completed. You can do that in five pound increments if you have a lot of weight to lose. That was just an example. What are you going to do to accomplish that goal? I'm going to exercise as soon as I wake up in the morning. I'm going to drink 8 glasses of water per day. I'm going to keep track of what I eat, and follow a specific food plan. Write it all down. What are your specific steps that you're going to do in order to have and achieve what you want to achieve? You can use the same process for any goal that you set.

Now the M in smack. When you are going to put the smack down on your goal you need to be motivated. The thing that motivates you more than anything else in the world is your reason why you want to do something. If you don't have a strong reason why, you probably won't achieve your goals and here's why. You have to want something so badly in your life that you get to the point where you say, "I cannot stand not having this in my life anymore."

Your why needs to be out there in front of you. You need to focus on your why. Make your why so desirable that you get emotional thinking about it. Make your reason why, the reason you get up in the morning.

Let me tell you exactly why I wrote this book. It took a long time, it took a lot of energy, it took money, it took commitment, it took integrity, it took focus, it took a lot of things that are a challenge, but I embraced those challenges because my why is huge. I woke up one day, and I realized something. I realized that someday, hopefully many, many years from now, I'm not going to be here anymore. On the day I die, I'm going to take with me what's in my head. I realized that, God forbid, if that happens sooner rather than later, the information that I have in my head would not be left behind for my children or anyone else. That scared me. That realization, that reason why, got me motivated. I'm telling you, the thought of leaving this earth without leaving this information for my children was terrifying to me. It was more motivating than anything else I've ever done in my life.

I also realized it wasn't just for my children, it was for you and your children and their children. I believed that I could write a book that could change someone's world. I believed I could influence people around the globe to start taking action and creating the life they want to live, and to me that vision was extraordinary. I knew I could influence people I've never met before through these words, and my influence on them would cause a chain reaction. I also knew that if I influenced them to take actions that made the lives of their families better, than I was influencing even more people. Then if those people went and influenced more people than I am in essence influencing more people. I started to see my positive influence happening all around the world but I had to do something. I had to write this book, so that was my specific goal. Write a book that would teach people how to design and live the life they want to live, step-by-step, moment by moment, goal by goal.

I was motivated by my why. My biggest why was because if I didn't do this I felt like I was cheating my children. I would tell my children, "Anything is possible." Nevertheless, I needed to provide a way to teach my children how to design their lives before I lost the ability to do it personally for some unforeseen reason. My 'why' continues to motivate me every day. Me, wanting a better life not only for myself and my children, but me wanting a better life for you and your children and their children, motivates me. So motivate yourself with a strong reason why.

Now the A is achieving. You need to be achieving steps along the way. You wrote them down. You said specifically what you are going to do. You may have created a step like, lose 1 pound, and you continued adding in that step for as many pounds as you want to lose. You now have a specific, motivating goal that you can see you are achieving. You will achieve those steps consistently. When you're achieving those steps, mark them off. Check them off your list. When you check off the steps on your list, by taking the specific actions you need to take, that will continue to motivate you.

Now be committed. I don't want you to be interested in creating your life. I don't want you to be interested in achieving your goals. I want you to be committed. The C in putting the smack down on your goals is committing. In order to commit to something, you have to decide when you are going to do it? You might decide, every day I'm going to get up at 6 o'clock in the morning and work on my goals. Every day after work I'm going to commit to going to the gym to lose the twenty pounds I am committed to losing. You have to commit to get what you want.

That's the mindset you have to have. You commit a time to work on that specific goal. Think of a goal that you might have set previously. Maybe you didn't commit to it and set up a time line to achieve that goal. Is it done yet? I'm going to guess probably not because you didn't commit a time to it. So commit, decide when you are going to work on and complete this goal. Set a timer and stay focused on one task for that time. Set a deadline on your calendar, and mark down how many days you have left. Each day you'll see how many days you have left to achieve your goal and that keeps your brain working. Your brain says, "I have to get to work; I have to do this now. I've got to start putting things into momentum and move things around to make it happen for you." By committing to your goal you allow your brain and the universe to work with you, to be on your side, you have friends, you have teammates, you have partners, and you have the universe that wants you to achieve your goals. The universe praises and rewards people who know specifically what they want. So commit to it.

You can do all those things. You can be specific, you can be motivated, you can achieve, you can commit to a time, but if you don't Keep going then what happens? The same thing that has always happened, will happen again. The New Year's resolutions, the someday, the I'll get to it, the I am interested goals. You might find yourself saying "I know, I should be doing that, but my show is on right now and I'm going to watch television instead." If you let things get in the way of your commitments, you stop moving. You don't have to be going 24 hours a day, seven days a week, always saying I can't sleep, I can't stop, I've got to go, I have goals to achieve, I have things to do. You don't have to be like that, however, you do need a sense of urgency in your goal.

Your goal might not be to change the world. I'm not telling you that you have to change the world with your goal but I am telling you that this is your life. Your goals need to be personal to you. This is the one time that you'll be on this earth and it's the one time you have to achieve whatever it is you want to achieve and influence who it is you want to influence. So use your time effectively, use it wisely, and keep moving.

Here are just a couple of last points on goal setting and goal achieving. I want you to be setting yourself up to win right now. I want you to always know you can achieve the goal you set, even if it stretches you. Nothing is unachievable in life, whatever you believe, you can achieve. I understand that, and I hope that you understand that too. However, when you set a goal, you need to ask if that goal is realistic for you? Only you can really answer that question. I want you to set yourself up to win. If you set unrealistic goals for yourself in the short term then you're not going to achieve them and failing to achieve milestones is not going to keep you motivated. Achieving, consistently, keeps you motivated. So when you set your goals, don't set them so far out that you aren't motivated. Set short-term, motivating, achievable goals as you are beginning to create your life.

What's the key to long term goal success? Take a long term goal, a huge goal, something you want wholeheartedly for your life, and break that goal down into specific smaller steps. We're going to cover a technique for doing this later. For now, just think, if your goal is to motivate 1 million people to achieve their goals, and you say, "That's what I want, specifically, okay, universe, hook me up, make it happen, put a million people in my path so I can influence them, so I can show them how to change their lives, and create everything they wanted, and achieve their goals." Is that a realistic goal short-term? No, but you can say "Okay my short-term goal is to create a product and sell that product to 10 people." That's realistic isn't it? Absolutely it is. Isn't that also motivating to know that you can change the lives of 10 people if you want to? Heck, yeah it is. That's motivating, that's specific. What about a larger milestone goal of helping 100 people?

How do you achieve that? Sell 5 of them, sell 10 of them, sell 50 more, and sell 100 of them. Boom, you're motivated, because you are achieving. When are you going to do that by? Are you going to do that by next year at this specific time? Commit to it and keep going. Remember, creating the life you want and living life at the level you desire is nothing more than creating goals, achieving those goals, and doing that over and over and over again. So like I said in the beginning, I want to teach you how to create and achieve one goal. Because once you do, everything else is possible. Everything else becomes achievable. You start to see grander and grander visions of what's possible in your life and I don't know what that is for you, only you can decide. It's your life and I want you to live it to its fullest. I want you to make the choice of what you want in your life, what goals you want to achieve, and then I want you to put the smack down on those goals.

Time Management

What's the number one reason why people say they won't achieve their goals? Because they say, "I don't have the time." There's a lot of other reasons like, "I don't have the money, I don't have the skills, I don't have the right tools." There are a lot of reasons why people say they can't achieve their goals, but the number one reason is time. People believe they don't have the time. But that's not true! That is a thought, which is a belief.

Are you telling me that people who achieve extraordinary amounts of success in their life, have everything they ever wanted, create the life they want to live, do the things they need to do to achieve everything they want to achieve are different? Are you telling me they have more time than you? Go ahead and try to win that one. It's all the same, universal across the board. No matter how hard you try to change it, unless you come up with a new way to measure time, you have 24 hours in your day, seven days in your week, 365 days in your year, and so does every single person on this earth, it's how we measure time.

The difference is how people manage their time. If you're not achieving what you want to achieve and you are saying it's because you don't have the time, it's because you are spending your time ineffectively. Time management isn't about filling up your day planner, minute by minute, second by second, knowing exactly what you're going to do every single moment of every single day. That doesn't work! Time management is about effectively using the time that you do have to really focus on what matters. It's about finding little pockets of time to focus on doing what you want to do. It's about finding the most efficient way to do things. That is time management. It's all a matter of moments!

I'm not only going to teach you time management. I told you just a little while ago I'm going to teach you how to create time. How much time do you want in your life right now? I'll show you how to create it. Do you need six days to accomplish your goal, you got it. Do you need a month, you got it. I'm going to show you exactly how to create time in your life, but I can't do it for you. I can only show you how. You have to create your time. I'm not the type of guy who says every single moment of every single day you need to be doing something, but the reality is, you are busy at every moment of every day. It's just a matter of figuring out what you're busy doing. I'm not sure how you've been spending your moments. I do know that seconds add up to minutes, minutes add up to hours, into days, into months, into years and all that time adds up to your lifetime. Your time is ticking by and you don't get it back.

We all have obligations, I get it, like I said I have five kids, I'm married, I have a busy life. I fully understand, you're busy. Don't start saying, "You don't know me, you don't know what I've got going on, I've got 4 jobs, I've got 12 kids, and I don't have time to do anything for myself." That's a lie. You're lying to yourself. Yes, you're busy, I don't doubt that, but again, I'm not here to allow you to make excuses anymore. I'm not here to lie to you and tell you that you can achieve anything you want to achieve in a short amount of time either. The less available time you do have because of your obligations the longer it might take you to achieve your goals, but does that give you an excuse not to work on them, as consistently as possible? No. If you don't like that, if you don't like that I'm going to push you to accomplish your goals, then I'm sorry, this book is not for you. I hope that you're the kind of person who says, "This is what I need. This is what I want in my life. I want somebody that says do it, get it done, and holds me accountable. And when I don't do it, they say, why not?"

I'm not going to tell you to do it and get it done without giving you the frame work that goes along with achieving your goals. I'm giving you the frame work and the tools as you read this right now, you just need to pay attention, and implement the tools. I'm not going to allow you to say, "I didn't do it, I guess I'm a failure, I guess I really don't have the time, or the desire, or the ability." That's not true, those are thoughts, and those are your beliefs if you allow them to be. Don't do that to yourself. When you find yourself criticizing, self-doubting, or sabotaging your own success, stop. Take a breath and allow yourself to think a new, positive, encouraging thought about something you want to believe.

A realization came for me when I got disgusted about not achieving the things I wanted to achieve. I got scared, I thought, wow, I'm wasting a lot of time in my life. When I started to look at how much time I was wasting, that really bothered me. I wanted to leave behind something of value for the world and if I wasn't using the time I had, I wasn't being true to myself, I wasn't being committed, and I wasn't living with integrity. I wasn't doing everything I could to make the lives of my family and the world a better place. That scared and bothered me. Now, let's look at some examples of how I was missing out on some very valuable time and maybe how you are too.

Are you sleeping too much? I understand, we need to sleep, but don't overdo it. You don't need 10 hours of sleep. If you have the ability to get 10 hours of sleep, and still accomplish your goals, well God bless you. You must be amazing at time management if you can sleep that much and still get everything done. If you're not getting everything done, remember, there are things in your life that can be getting done during that time you are over sleeping.

I'm going to show you a staggering number that should wake you up. How old are you? Take the amount of years that you've been alive and divide that by three. Go ahead and do the math right now.

My age _____ divided by 3 = _____ years I've slept.

That's the amount of years you've slept in your life if you only sleep 8 hours each night. I'm not telling you to deprive yourself of sleep. If you do, you won't function right, your emotions won't work right, your brain won't work right, your physical ability to get things done won't be the same as if you rest and you get the right amount of sleep. How much sleep do you need? Only you know that for yourself. So don't feel like I'm saying, don't sleep, don't ever sleep, drink coffee, stay up all night long and get your goals done. I'm not saying that but I'm saying don't overdo it. Commit to a time you are going to get up every day and stick to it, no matter what.

How much television do you watch? According to Nielsen, the company that monitors people's television habits, the average person spends more than four hours every single day watching television, that's 28 hours per week, that's two full months of your time every single year. If you only live 65 years and you watch four hours of television every day you will spend nine years of your life watching television! What are you watching anyway? You're watching other people live and create their lives. You watch other people live the life that maybe you want to live but instead of doing what it takes you're living your reality through their reality and the whole time your life is going by. Now I like to watch some television. I like to watch movies. When I started to realize how much time we waste sitting in front of the television, on the couch, not doing anything else at that time, I realized that is a lot of time I'd be wasting. So again, remember, I am not the person who tells you to throw away your television. Yes, some people might realize how much time they are wasting and say, "I'm getting rid of my television, I don't want it, I don't need it, good bye, see you later," and they do. If you decide to do that, go for it, do whatever you need to do. What I'm asking you to do is be more aware of the time you spend in front of the television, because the amount of time you spend there is the amount of time you're not spending working on creating and achieving your goals. You can have the t.v. on and still do something else, that's fine. But if you do that you're not really focused on doing the things that you want to do. So just be aware that things like watching television can be wasting valuable time that at some point you'll wish you had back. I would bet, once you begin to focus on what matters to you, you'll begin wanting to spend less time doing unproductive things.

How about games on your phone or other devices? Are you playing a lot of games instead of working on things that actually matter in your life? Could you be focusing screen time on things that make a difference in how you feel, how you look, how you influence this world? Games are addicting because they give you a sense of accomplishment. However, they waste valuable time that can be used accomplishing things that actually matter in your life. Monitor your time. Be realistic, be honest with how much time you're spending playing games.

How about driving? Well, of course you have to drive right? You have to drive to work, you have to drive to the store, you have to drive the kids around, you spend a lot of time driving but if you're just driving, you are wasting precious time. How about taking the time when you're driving, to listen to an audio program. Your library probably has audio downloads you can borrow for free. You can download the audio books for free and then put them on your phone, computer, or whatever you use and listen to them in your car. There are sites like audible.com and learnoutloud.com where you can download audio books on whatever you want to learn. Use that time wisely. Every day when you are commuting to work can be used to learn a skill you need to advance, or change your career.

How about social media like facebook and twitter or any of the other time wasters. All the time people spend on there, not only playing games but reading about other people's lives, reading about what other people are doing, is wasted time. Social media is a part of our life in this modern day way of communicating. I'm not telling you to eliminate social media from your life. What I'm suggesting is to monitor your time. We all know it's possible when you jump on facebook an hour goes by. If you're going to be someone who is focused on achieving your goals then you have to be aware of that time.

Now what about really short bits of time. What about when you pop something in the microwave, you set the timer for a minute and you stand there waiting, watching the food go around, waiting for it to, ding! That's time. That's time that you can use. What can you do during those moments? How about waiting for the coffee to brew or the water to boil? Little bits of time add up, so if you can find little things to do during your time, that are going to move you in the direction of achieving your goals then use those times. That's effective time management.

My dad had a plaque hanging in our garage when I was a kid. I understood it and I got it but not at the level I do now. The plaque said this, "I must do the most productive thing possible at every given moment." Now, at the time… I didn't really understand what the sign meant. I really didn't get that what was written on that plaque was time management in and of itself. We have moments and in those moments of our lives we need to decide what is the most productive thing you can be doing at that moment. So that sign, I must do the most productive thing

62

possible at every given moment, means use your time wisely. Don't allow those seemingly small moments of time to add up. Again, I'm not saying you need to quit your job, never sleep, and smash your television. I'm not telling you to do those things. I hope you're not taking what I'm saying as "You're a bum because you watch t.v," that's not what I'm saying. I really just want to make you aware of how time adds up and solidify the fact that time is our most valuable asset.

People spend years going to school, and even more time going to college. They spend lots of money, and they learn something they might enjoy doing, hopefully. People do this, knowing they're going to spend a third of their life doing this type of work if they choose it as a career. That's a huge commitment. Are you working a job you just don't like? Even if you do like it, I'm asking if it's your passion and your purpose in life? Do you have the desire to do something else with your life but you feel like you're just kind of stuck working that job? Well how many years have you been working? Divide that by three and that's how many years you've been working toward helping someone else to build their goals, and build their dream life. You obviously need money to survive, so you need to work to produce an income. What I'm asking you though, is do you have the desire to change your life's work, to create the life you want? If so, you can't allow an excuse like, "I'm too busy at work" to get in your way. You can't allow that to be an excuse for why you're not creating a plan to move you towards the job or career you would really like to have.

How about using the time you drive to and from work, to listen to an audio book on how to do what you want to do. Do you listen to books on goal setting, on mindset, on achievement, use drive time to live the life you want to live because you're finding and creating the pockets of time that you need. You could use that half hour you're driving to work, and the half hour you are driving home. That's an hour a day you can focus on learning exactly what it is you want to learn. How about learning how to create a business you have been wanting to create over the next year. Take that hour a day, which you do have, and listen to someone who's already done it. I guarantee there is something out there, there is an audio program you can buy that's a lot less expensive than college that you can listen to while you're driving or working out or making dinner for everybody, that can help you fulfill that goal.

You don't have to be one hundred percent fully engaged in driving your car at all times. You need to be aware, but what I'm saying is that the same way you can listen to music and drive; you can listen to an audio program and drive. You can listen to audios while you're making dinner and the kids are playing or whatever is going on around you. You don't need to be fully engaged in what's happening around you. You can use those times to listen and to learn. So if you were to take the next year, an hour a day, you would give yourself three hundred and sixty five hours of information. Now that's using your time wisely. Focus on getting a job you know you would enjoy if you don't want to start a business. If your goal is to just get the exact job you want you can take the time to learn what you need to learn.

I get it, some employers do require that you have a bachelor's degree. However, some of them, if you have the knowledge, the skills, the willingness to learn, and the desire to make their company better will take a serious look at you. If you've learned on your own over a period of time by reading and studying about that particular company and you know exactly what the company is all about then you can still apply. If you know what they produce, exactly how they do what they do, you're familiar with the processes and systems the company uses, you are just as qualified as some other candidates, maybe more! If you have specific knowledge of the industry, who do you think they are going to take a real serious look at compared to a young college kid who just graduated and has a general education degree, the same as all the other applicants have? If you said to them, "I took the last year while I was working full time and I studied exactly what your company does because I have wanted to work for you for a long time. I know exactly how you produce your results, how you use your systems and exactly how to manufacture your product. I know how your management system works, I can see how the sales and the production lines work and I learned everything I could about your business. I'm asking for an opportunity to work for you because I am passionate about what you do." How do you think that they would look at you? Are they going to say "But you don't have a bachelor's degree?" They're not necessarily going to say that to you. You won't know unless you approach them. Create your life. Create the life that you want to live. They might tell you, "I'm sorry, one of our requirements is to have a bachelor's degree." If that's the case, you have to then make the choice of whether or not to go back to school and get your bachelor's degree. I can't make those choices for you. Only you can.

What I'm telling you is that there are times in your life where you can use the time you have available more effectively. Instead of wasting time on social media, how about going on YouTube and instead of watching pointless videos, watch videos from someone who can inspire you and teach you what you want to learn. There's so much information out there. The time you're wasting playing games, watching television or any other dream killer could be used to exercise, to read a book, to play with your kids or learn a new skill. Do the math, add it up and be honest with yourself. How much time are you spending doing things that waste your time. You'll probably have a consciousness awakening and get pretty disgusted by it.

Start to multiply it. How much does this 20 minutes a day that I'm spending doing this, equal over a year? What can I do to replace that activity? How can I use my time more effectively in order to create and live the life I want? How about those little times that we talked about, like putting something in the microwave. Be aware of that time and use it to do those 10 push-ups, 10 lunges, or 10 squats. Maybe you can do a whole set, 20 seconds of push-ups, 20 seconds of squats, 20 seconds of lunges, 20 seconds of dips on the counter, there are so many little things that you can do in that short amount of time while you're waiting for the microwave to, ding. You'll start to realize these things now that you're aware of them.

When do you read your affirmations? Couldn't you print out a list of your affirmations, tape them on your microwave or even put them in a nice frame and hang them behind the microwave or on a close wall. Stand there and focus on your affirmations. Whatever your affirmations are, read them, focus on them. Use that time, don't just stand there, do something.

But sometimes the opposite is true. Sometimes the most effective use of your time is to do absolutely nothing. Sometimes the most effective use of your time is to sit and breathe, meditate, or pray. Get yourself into a positive mindset by focusing on positive thoughts. Sometimes the most effective use of your time is to sleep. In that instance, don't just do something, sit there. Allow your body to relax. Use the time you have to effectively create your life. If you're exhausted, don't keep doing things. You're not going to do them with the same ability as you would have if you are well rested. So get an extra hour of sleep, take a nap or just get a few hours of sleep and let your brain recover. So either, don't just stand there, do something, or don't just do something, sit there. Sit there and enjoy the peace and quiet. That might clear your brain. Don't just do something, get some rest. Don't just do something, meditate and breathe and be in the moment. Don't just do something, pray, and ask God to heighten your awareness of His purpose for your life.

How you use your time is completely up to you. Here are some more ideas for you. If your goal is to lose twenty pounds, please don't drive around the parking lot wasting minutes looking for the closest parking spot. Don't do that! Get the spot way in the back of the parking lot and use those few minutes to walk briskly inside. Then, when you are shopping, walk around, don't drive one of those little carts around because you are obese. When you are finished checking out walk briskly all the way to the back of the parking lot curling the bags like hand weights the whole way and put the things in your car. That's effectively using your time. Don't worry about how you look, you're being effective and I bet you'll inspire someone else to do the same!

Now listen, I understand, if you're handicapped, if you have a physical disability and you need to find a close parking spot because you're limited in your mobility, you're not the person I'm talking to. I'm talking to the excuse makers who are overweight because they are eating too much and they are not moving enough. I've been one of those people a few times in life! These are ways that you can incorporate exercise and calorie burning into your life within your daily activities. Instead of spending those couple minutes driving around waiting for someone to pull out of a parking spot so you can get it, find a spot and walk a bit. How about getting off the bus, if you take the bus to work, get off a block or two earlier and walk. One minute more, one minute less, in the grand scheme of your daily life isn't going to make much difference. But one minute more and one minute less over the course of a year, adding all of those additional steps into your routine, makes a huge difference. People just don't use bits of time effectively.

Now, how do you actually find the time if you simply don't have time? I know you might still be saying to yourself, "Hey, this sounds great but you don't know what else I'm dealing with. When I get out of the car, I've got four kids that I've got to get into the store. I'm not going to be able to drag them all the way through the parking lot because I want to get a burn on. It's not going to happen in my life. Tell me something I can use in my life...." I can't. I can't tell you how to effectively use your time. I can tell you how to manage your time. You have to make the best use of your moments and everyone is going to do that differently.

What is time management? It's simply a choice of how to use the moments of your life for what matters most to you. Time, in the physical sense, doesn't actually exist. We simply use a clock and a calendar as a way of meeting up at specific moments of our life. We don't actually have time, we have moments in our life and we corresponded those moments with other people in a system we refer to as time. What you really need to focus on is moment management, because moments are real! I certainly understand you have obligations and needs that eat into your time. You need to sleep and work and you probably have other things in your life that require your time. What you do have though is "Your" time. Everyone does. At any moment of your life, you are either using your time for yourself or you are using your time for someone else.

So if everyone has the same amount of time in life, then what happens? If you're giving your time to someone, and if they're taking your time, they're using your time. If you're using your time to fill their time, they are effectively using your time. Do you want other people to use your time? Do you have more than enough time to just give it away? The same works the opposite way. If someone is using their time for you, then you are effectively using someone else's time to your advantage. There is always a give and take of time at every moment of your life.

Now, time management is not easy. There is a big difference between easy and simple. What I'm teaching you how to do is look at your life in a simpler way. In order to use your time, you have to learn how to say no to other things and other people who are using your time. When you say no to other people and other things, who are you saying yes to? You're saying yes to yourself. Most people have a really hard time saying yes to themselves for what matters, but they say yes to themselves at the wrong times by doing the wrong things. So when it comes time for someone else to want your time, you say, "I never have any of my own time." That's because you may be using your time ineffectively. So when you want time for yourself, you don't have it because you wasted it.

Then somebody else comes to you and they say, "Can I have some time please," and you think, "My life is filled with pleasing other people, I never have time for myself, I have to use all my time for them." That's not true. If you're using your time effectively, you can balance your time but if you're wasting your time you're going to feel spread out, overwhelmed by time, and frustrated. You're going to feel like you have no time for yourself.

It's not selfish to take your time for yourself if you're using it to better your life. If you're using it to better your life and you're making the lives of those around you better in the process, that's not selfish. But if you are using your time playing games, going on social media, watching useless shows on television, gossiping on the phone, or doing other non productive things then you are wasting your time, and other's time, by not giving quality time to those who want some of your time.

You also need to practice balancing your time. If you spend all your time with your family and you have a business you want to grow, then you are going to have a really strong family but you're going to have a really weak business. If you spend all your time working on your business, you will have a really strong business that's growing but you're going to have a family that's falling apart. You've got to learn to balance. Take a little time from here, and put it there. Take a little of their time, let them have a little of your time. Find pockets here and there and use the time you have effectively.

How do you know what to do during those times? You create a specific plan. If you have a goal that is specific and you have specific action steps you know you need to take, have a to do list of those action items. Maybe you have to make a phone call that will take no more than a couple of minutes, the next time you have two minutes and wonder what you should do, DO THAT, mark it off your list. Achieve it. You're one step closer to accomplishing your goals. This takes practice, this takes commitment, and this takes being hyper aware of what you are doing each moment.

You can do this. Do it. Do it starting now!

Create 'You' Time

I will (do)

_____

Every (day/time)_____

I will (do)

_____

Every (day/time)_____

I will (do)

_____

Every (day/time)_____

I will (do)

_____

Every (day/time)_____

I will (do)

_____

Every (day/time)_____

The Story Of Some People

I know there are going to be some people who really get this and apply the information. Some people are going to say, "I know exactly where I've been wasting my time. How I'm using words in a disempowering way, and why I've not been succeeding in my goals." I also know that there are going to be some people that don't get it. They don't get what I'm saying. I'm a very realistic person, like I said, and I know some people are going to focus and take what they have learned, and create the life they want to live. They're going to start using the ABC's Of Success, the affirmations, and the 'be, do, have' pattern of achieving what they want. They are going to use effective goal setting, and they're going to use time management effectively. Then I know there are going to be other people who will not do these things.

Here is a funny example of what some people will do at this point in the book. Picture a 'Talker' type of person in your mind and imagine them saying this...

"I've got this, I know how I can be rich. I've already got the belief, I believe it, so I've got the perfect foundation. Time management, that's a joke. Time management's no problem. I know exactly how to combine my activities. My goal, simple, *be* rich! What am I going to do? I'm going to, be rich! What else do I have to *do*, I'm going to be rich! I know what I'm going to have. I'm going to *have* a yacht, and a mansion, and a Ferrari, and a hot spouse! Want to know how? Let me show you how I'm going to do it. I already set my goal, look, it's right there…I am going to be rich! How much more specific can I be? Here's the steps I'm going to take. You can see it. First, I'm going to buy a Ferrari. I've always wanted a Ferrari. Then I'm going to buy a mansion. I'm going to buy it on the water, so I can have my yacht right outside my house."

"So, those are my steps. I'm going to buy the Ferrari, then the mansion, then the yacht. I believe that I'm going to do that in one year and here's how. I know that I have to focus on exactly what I want, so I went through the tv programs and I found those shows that have the mega yachts, and the mansions. You've probably seen those shows. Well, I've set those shows up to record on my dvr. Not only that, there are lavish vacation shows and all of that is what I'm setting to record. So, when I watch those shows my brain is going to say, 'that's what he wants, I'm going to get it for him.' The universe is going to know it, because I'm specific, I'm clear, and I'm so motivated, because I've never had money before. I'll tell you, money motivates me."

"I've done it, I've set the specific goal to be rich, my steps are Ferrari, mansion, yacht. I'm motivated by my why because I'm motivated by money and I'm committed to doing this and having this in one year. This is amazing, I'm so glad I got this book. Time management, are you kidding, that stuff is so easy. I know how to be good at time management. Here's how I'm going to manage my time. I'm going to update my status and tell everybody what I'm going to do, while I'm watching those shows, that's two things at once. While I type with my right hand, I'm going to eat with my left hand. So, I'm watching the show, posting online, and eating at the same time. I'm doing three things at once. I'm so good at this time management thing that I don't think I even need the rest of this book. I don't think Tom even knows what he's talking about. He only talks about doing a couple things at once, I'm doing three."

"But here's the real kicker. Yesterday I was adding up how much time I was spending at work and I said, wow, I'm spending 8 hours at work every day. I did the math, I added it up, 8 hours every day, that's 2080 hours this year that I'm wasting at a job I hate. So I quit my job, I did it, I quit my job yesterday and I'm going to use those 8 hours effectively. I'm going to focus on watching those shows and I'm going to believe that everything's possible. Man, this law of attraction thing is awesome! I'm only going to focus on watching shows that show exactly what I want. I bet it won't even take me a year. I bet if I really focus and play the lottery and don't let anyone distract me from watching all my shows, I bet it won't even take me a year to get it!"

"After I have all those things, I'm going to go out and find the hottest person that you have ever seen. They will be so attracted to me. I'm going to use that law of attraction to attract people to me and I'm going to marry the one I want. I'll probably have to choose between several since everyone will want me. Once we're married, we're going to have two kids, I think we're going to have a boy and a girl, maybe twins, I don't know cause I haven't figured that out exactly yet. Once we have those two kids, I've already decided that on Christmas morning I'm going to surprise them with a cute little puppy that we'll put under the tree. They're going to be so excited. You know what the dog's name is going to be? We're going to name the dog Action so the kids will learn that you have to take Action for a walk in order to get what you want in life! Don't I have such a good plan for my life? I'm going to stop reading and give this book to someone who actually needs it right now. There's no reason for me to keep reading, I've got this! I'm so excited about my life right now."

I know, that example is pretty outrageous, but, I'm hoping that you see, that's how some people are. Some people are excited, they have all the enthusiasm, they have all the energy, but, they aren't doing what they need to do. All they ever do is talk about improving their life. They really believe they can have everything they want in their life. But, they are not taking the actions necessary, consistently over time, to have what they want. Do you see how the ABC's Of Success are really everything you need, to have what you want in your life?

Don't be that person. Please! Don't just sit around believing that somehow a huge check will show up in your mailbox. Don't quit your job because it's going to allow you to have more time. Don't believe all you have to do is "Use the law of attraction" and you'll get what you want. That's nothing more than a marketing ploy to get you to buy a program. Do, use the time you have efficiently and work toward your goal by taking the steps necessary over a period of time.

Now, here's the last thing I want you to understand about time management. My goal and my purpose for creating a time management section within the ABC's Of Success, is for you to understand, your time is extraordinarily valuable. Time comes with opportunity and opportunity will pass you by if you don't value your time. The opportunities of our lives don't stick around forever. Opportunity looks for people who are opportunistic. They say, "There's an opportunity. I'm taking it." Now, certainly there are people who are opportunistic and they take advantage of people. That is not the opportunistic that I'm talking about. I'm saying, if you have the opportunity to do something in the moment, right now, because that's the time it's happening in your life, well then be aware of it and do it.

If you have kids, those kids are only young once. The opportunity to enjoy them, spend time with them, teach them your values and beliefs, play with them, show them how much you love them, that opportunity is happening right now. If you are young and your time is not limited by the family obligations some other people have, use that to your advantage. So if that's you and you are ambitious enough to say, "I want to create the life I want to live," have the courage, the energy and the enthusiasm to do so, because your life may change unexpectedly. One thing definitely will change, you will get older, time will pass you by, and once that time passes by, you do not get it back. We get one opportunity at each moment of our lives. When you let those moments pass you by, you let opportunity pass you by. All we have in our lives are a whole lot of moments, one after the other. Eventually our moments disappear and our opportunities disappear with them and when they disappear, they disappear forever. They may come back again, you might have a second opportunity, but you will never have that first opportunity again.

Once again, that realization scared me on a massive level. I literally got scared I would run out of time. I feared I would run out of time and I wouldn't leave this information behind for people, and that scared me. So, it's your life. What do you want in your life? Is it a feeling? Is it a feeling of being loved? Is it giving love? Is it giving opportunity to others? Is it extraordinary wealth? Is it a cleaner environment? Is it new ideas and inventions? I don't know. That's for you to figure out. It's your life. You have one chance, one opportunity to live it. Now use the time you have and leave behind what you choose to leave behind.

I also understand that you might not know what you want to leave behind. You might say, "I want to leave something behind but I just don't know what." Don't worry. You are using your time wisely right now by reading this book, because I am going to help you figure out what you want to be doing. I told you, trust me, I will not leave you longing for more and saying, "That didn't give me what I wanted." Everything you want for your life is going to be possible. You just have to identify it and take the actions necessary. We're going to do all of those things throughout the series of books in Your Journey Of Being.

I want you to start practicing something as we finish up this section on time management. Remember when we talked about the 'be, do, have' pattern? I want you to start asking yourself a simple question, each moment of your life. For instance if you have an argument on your hands, then you need to ask yourself this question. If you have some down time, you have to ask yourself this question. If you are getting what you want and want to keep having success, ask this question. If you have a choice that has to be made, then you have to ask yourself this question. The question is this. "Who what or how am I being?" Then you give yourself this answer. "I am being, *what*?" Who what or how are you being at that moment? If you are having an argument, are you being argumentative? If you have a choice to make, are you being decisive or are you being wishy washy? If you have some time on your hands, are you being effective with your time, or are you being lazy? If you are being treated the way you want to be treated, pay attention! How are you being? Your life is going to move in a certain direction based on how you are being.

When you begin to ask yourself this question and answer it honestly you are going to begin to see a shift in how you approach your life. So let's just say that you are having an argument and you say, "Who, what or how am I being?" You realize that you are being close minded, selfish, and argumentative. Well, what is that getting you? What do you have because of what you are being? Do you have an argument on your hands with someone you actually love and don't like to argue with? What do you want to have? Do you want to have love, and peace, and a nice conversation?

When you are aware of how you are being in various situations, ask yourself another question. Ask yourself, "Who, what or how would I have to be in order to get what I want?" So if you want to have a nice conversation with the person you are now having an argument with, how would you have to be in order to have what you want? Would you have to be more open minded? Would you have to be more understanding? Would you have to be more loving? If you were being loving, understanding, and compassionate, do you think you would have a nicer conversation? I bet you would. If you are being more loving, compassionate, understanding, open minded, patient, and a good listener, then would you be listening and really hearing what the other person has to say? Would you be using a calmer tone of voice? Would you be looking in the person's eyes, maybe holding their hand? Would you be listening to what they are telling you from their perspective on life? Would you be being open minded and accepting that your point of view is just your point of view. What would you be doing in order to have the conversation you want to have?

So, get used to asking that question of yourself. When you answer, why you have what you have will become clear to you. That question is only effective if you are honest with yourself. If you lie to yourself then you are probably going to continue to have what you have. The more open and honest you can be with yourself and with others, in the moments of your life, will make a major difference in how your life goes. Moments are opportunities. Ask yourself that question at each moment. If you don't have, or are not getting what you want, then you can say, "what would I need to do in order to be who I need to be in order to have what I want to have?" Those three things are going to start allowing you to create your life in this moment. Start to learn to ask yourself that question often and watch what happens.

Watch What Happens

Watch what happens when you start to identify who, what and how you are being in the present moments of your life. You are going to begin to awaken a whole new sense of being present and living life in the moment, as it is happening. Let me ask you a question. Could you imagine what your life would be like, if everyone around you was asking themselves that question at every moment of their lives? Imagine your boss was asking himself, how am I being? What am I being? Who am I being? If I want to have the company I want to have, what would I have to do for my employees, for my business? What would I have to do in the company itself in order to have the company I want?

What about your spouse? Your friends? Your kids? What if at every moment they were asking themselves, "Who, what, and how am I being right now that is creating the life I have?" In this moment, at this time, what everyone has right now in their life is a result of how they are being. If everyone asked themselves that question and they answered the question with honesty, they would realize why they have what they have. If they said "I don't want that in my life, I want this in my life," then they would have to say, "How would I need to be, who would I need to be, what would I need to be, in order to have that?" When they are innately aware of the answer to the question, they would immediately do what they needed to do, in that moment, to change what they have. Could you imagine if everyone in the world did that? It's possible. But it is only possible if they know what you now understand.

We are just getting started, we're just warming up, but I can imagine you are probably seeing your life in a way you have never seen it before. Imagine if the people in your life could read just the first few chapters of this book. What do you think your life would be like as a result of them having this information? Do you think that your life would be better as a result of the people around you knowing and having the understanding of what you now have? If they knew how time management really works, about how they can put the smack down on their goals, and about what kind of mindset they can have. Do you think you would benefit from the knowledge they would gain? Imagine they knew to ask themselves how they are being and what they need to do so they can have what they want. How would your life be if they now understood this information?

If you want the people in your life to have this information, so *your* life improves, then share it with them. In today's world, people are quick to share, but often times, what they are sharing is not going to improve their world. I believe that this work, can in fact change the world for the better. I won't be able to do it as effectively if we don't work together though. I need your help to start a movement! My ultimate goal is for this work to be standardized education, so children learn it early in life. Just imagine a world where everyone approached every situation with the desire to make it better!

Here is what is really important. Do you think that you could effectively explain to them and get them to understand exactly what you now understand because I explained it to you in a step by step system? If you do, then by all means go ahead and spend an hour explaining to them exactly what you just learned. If you don't believe you would have the ability to effectively explain this to them, then I want you to share this book with them. I don't want you to explain to them the next time you are having an argument, that they are *being* defensive, *being* argumentative and *being* closed minded. I don't want you to tell them what they are doing wrong and that's why they are having an argument. That's not going to go well, it's just not.

What will work, is everyone in the world having access to this information when they need it. Imagine children, learning to put the smack down on their goals! Imagine a child, using "I am" statements from the time they learn how to write! Picture those children, learning to ask themselves "Who, what and how am I being that is contributing to what I have right now." In the course of a single generation, we would educate the world to think differently. This is not going to happen without some focused, intentional effort on the part of everyone. I'm just one man, without you, I am nothing. With you, we are everything! I'm asking for your help!

My job, is to show people how to overcome the obstacles in their life that hold them back from being who they were born to be. I love to show people how to blast through those blocks like they don't even exist because people have blocks, people have a lot of them. We are going to cover more of that in the book, The Next Level. I am going to show you why so many people don't live the life they want to live. More importantly, I'm going to show you exactly how to overcome every obstacle and how to live at your peak!

How you choose to share this information with people is up to you. In fact, people may begin to ask you what has changed about you. When that happens, I would love the opportunity to be their guide as well.

Please don't ever tell anyone that they need to read this book though. When you tell someone what they need, they are less likely to do it. If you want to encourage someone to read this book, be a positive influence in their life. Be the person who shows them how to get what they want in their life, like I'm going to do in your life.

If someone is struggling with something, and you believe this book can help them, just say "I just read about how to overcome that in a book I'm reading…." When they ask "What's the name of the book?" Tell them.

Change who, what, and how you are being by planning ahead right now.

Change your being

When I am being

_____

I will stop and (do)

_____

When I am being

_____

I will stop and (do)

_____

When I am being

_____

I will stop and (do)

_____

When I am being

_____

I will stop and (do)

_____

When I am being

_____

I will stop and (do)

_____

Associations

Now, who are those people in your life? Who are those people who might look at you and say, "You look different," or "I've never seen you do that before," or "What are you working on?" Well, those people are your associations. Those people are who you associate with at this time in your life. They are the people, places, and the things that you associate with and your associations are really important to recognize. You have to begin to recognize who, what, and where you are associating to know what is affecting your ability to achieve your goals. We are going to start with the biggest associations that you have which are the associations you have with other people.

Think back to when you were a kid. I hope that you had parents who did this, and if you are a parent, I hope you are doing this too. Your parents wanted to know who you were hanging out with. Your parents wanted to know who your friends were. Basically, what they wanted to know is who your associations were. They wanted to know who you were associating with in your life because those associations are going to affect your life. Those associations are going to have an influence on the type of person you become. Now your parents, hopefully, wanted you to associate with other kids who they saw as good associations, good influences on you, because those associations helped shape your character. If your parents noticed you were hanging out with kids that maybe didn't have the same values your parents were trying to instill in you, then your parents probably didn't want you to hang out with those people any more. They didn't want you to associate with those kids. As a parent, I'm looking at who my kids are associating with because who my kids associate with is going to shape and influence them in who they become.

Children are different than adults. Children are limited in their exposure. They can't make decisions and choices for themselves as easily as we can as adults. As adults we can pretty much choose whoever we want to hang out with. If you are associating with people in your life and those people don't have the type of life you want for yourself, well then you have to be aware of how those associations are affecting your life. Become aware of whether or not these people are living their lives in the way you want to live your life, and are they moving in the direction you want your life to go? If you want your life to move in a certain direction, are these people going to help you to get what you want just by the nature of who they are being? Answer that question honestly. Ask yourself if these people have any idea what they want in their life. More importantly, are they doing anything to get it? Are they a talker or are they a doer?

You might find the people you associate with most often have no idea what they want and they certainly aren't doing anything to get it. Don't blame them though, it's not their fault. They've never had the chance to learn what you are learning now. They've never been educated with anything more than the traditional educational system that never had them ask these questions, never asked them, "what do you want for your life?" Exactly what you want, not just

what job you want and not just what you want to do for your work
to get a paycheck. What do you want? I bet no one ever asked
them that question, especially in recent years. Now, here is what
I'm not telling you to do. I'm not telling you to leave your spouse,
dump your friends, and go live with the monks at the top of the
mountain because you want inner peace. You can have the people
in your life that you want to have in your life and begin to associate
with other people who are moving more in the direction you want
to go in.

A lot of the people you associate with right now might not be ready
for change in their lives. Some people are interested in living a
better life but they are not committed, and that's okay. Some
people might not believe a life different than what they have right
now is even possible, and that's okay too. You can't force people
to live a better life. You can only influence people by showing
them a better life is possible. Are you starting to see a connection
here? Everything we have discussed so far and everything we will
continue to discuss is all connected together to form life itself.
What you make of this life is up to you, and that is true for
everyone.

Everyone lives by their own beliefs. If someone's foundation of
belief is that their success in life is what they do for work, or their
life is defined by where they live, the car they have right now, and
what they do on a daily basis. If they believe that is what they
deserve to have in their life, then that's their foundational belief
system. That is what they build upon. It's just like neighborhoods.
Houses are built on similar foundations in similar areas. Houses
are associated with other similar houses. That's why you don't see
a new mansion being built in the middle of the ghetto. If you are
attempting to build your new foundation for an extraordinary life
in a neighborhood of other people whose foundations are not
appropriately suited for what you want to build, they are going to
break your windows and graffiti your new house and you're not
going to like living in that neighborhood.

I'm not saying you have to move to the rich neighborhood to succeed. I'm telling you that you should start associating with other people who are beyond your current associations. How do you do that? You begin by doing things like what you are doing right now, reading books on what you want to learn. Listening to the right audios on what you want to learn, going to seminars, joining the right groups online, watching the right videos, and reading the right blogs, books, and anything else you can do to get the right people in your head. These little things you do will allow you to start associating with the people who have the life you want to live. You want to know what they did in order to have what you want, and this will start putting you around people who are moving in the direction you want to go. So look at what you want and ask yourself, who is moving in that direction? If the people in your life aren't moving in that direction, you need to find people who are. Surround yourself with the people who have what you want or are at least moving in the direction of achieving their goals. Make sure those goals are in line with what you want.

What do you do if you are literally surrounded with people who are negative, unsupportive, or are not ambitious? Well, the first thing you need to do is really decide if the people that are in your life right now are the type of people you want to keep in your life. Do you really want them in your life anyway or do you need to start stepping away. Do you need to start disassociating with any of the people in your life? Don't 'diss' them, don't blow them off and be disrespectful, but disassociate yourself from the people you know are not good in your life.

You need to learn to be honest with yourself. Are they the type of people who are going to hang on to your leg while you're climbing toward the peak? Are they energy zombies limping through life with that bent over limp saying, "I've got no energy, I must ruin the lives of others to feel powerful." If they grab on to your leg and bite, you're going to turn into a zombie too, kick them off, and get rid of them! You don't want to be attacked by those energy zombies in your life. Those people are horrible! However, if they're not a complete energy zombie, then what do you do? You need to be open and honest with the people in your life. Have a conversation with them about what you want.

You can say to them, "Listen, I'm reading a book right now that has just opened my mind to a whole new realm of possibilities. I'm starting to identify exactly what I want for my life. I'm achieving goals I've never achieved before. I know the goals I want to achieve, I have more ambition, I have more clarity, I have more focus, I've learned time management skills and my belief system is through the roof right now. I have a vision for my future that I've never had before in my life!" Imagine having that conversation with a person when your conversation usually consists of, "Where do you feel like going for lunch, what are you doing later," or Work was horrible today." It's a little bit different, right? It is a little bit different of a conversation and that person is going to react in one of two ways.

Some people are going to say, "I want some of that, give me some, where do I get it," and they're going to want what you're on. You'll begin to see the people in your life differently when you finish this book, mainly because the people in your life will begin to see you differently. When you're high on life, some people will be really happy for you. That's the one way people might react. The other way people might react is to say, "You're an idiot. What the heck are you on. That's so stupid. You have never done things like that before. You've got to be kidding me right now, right?"

Here is what I want to warn you about. Those people could be the people that are closest to you. Those people might have your last name. Those people who are closest to you that are supposed to love you and support you and want you to live the best life possible, they might be your biggest negative associations. Those people suck the positive spirit out of you if you spend too much time around them. You've got to get rid of them. You've got to stop hanging around them. I understand, you can't just disown those people and I'm not telling you to write them out of your will. What I'm telling you is that you have to be honest with them and say, "I get it, I understand, you're not ready to take this new journey with me. I just wanted to let you know that I'm working on some goals right now and I didn't want you to think I was blowing you off." Don't waste your energy on those energy zombies. Don't try to reason with an energy zombie. You will get exhausted, they will overwhelm you, and then they'll bite at your face, rip your skin off, and turn you into an energy zombie too. Of course, that won't happen, but you know what I'm saying. You can't talk with a zombie and tell a them you found the cure for their zombiism. They don't listen, they don't hear it, and they don't understand it. You can't stand there and say, "wait a second, I know you don't have the energy, or ambition, or desire, or the drive to change your life right now but check this out." They're going to say, "No" and then they are going to chew your face off.

So for those people who are negative, for those people who are not going to support you, what you have to do is have a conversation about how they can support you. If you need to have that conversation about support with the person because they aren't willing to believe what you want is possible, then, again, you just say to them, "I understand, you are not ready to take this journey with me, I get it, but I've reached a point in my life where I need more. I've looked at my life and I realized I am not getting any younger and I haven't achieved what I want to achieve in my life. I have goals, I have desires, I have ambitions, and I haven't been doing the things that I have to do in order to have the life that I want to have. I cherish our friendship, I want you in my life, I really adore having you as a friend. I just want you to know that instead of going to the bar, going to happy hour, and doing all of the stuff we normally do after work, I've chosen to work on some goals I have for my life and I'm going to do that now every day after work. All I'm asking is that you support me. Just understand that I want something else for my life right now. Can you do that for me please?"

Hopefully they say yes but if not you have to realize that you have a zombie in disguise. If they're nasty with you and they get upset about it, then they aren't really a friend you want anyway, and maybe you need to rethink that friendship. But hopefully they'll say, "Yes, I can support you and I wish you the best. I really hope you achieve everything you want to achieve in your life." How do you get those people to eventually join you? You do what you want to do, you show them it's possible, and you continue to occasionally invite them. When they ask you how it's going, you say, "It's amazing, and I feel better than I've ever felt in my life." Then those people start to think maybe it is possible to live a more fulfilling life, maybe I do want that in my life.

When you make the choice to be successful, you are going to be able to identify those associations in your life that are holding you back. You have to be honest with yourself and then be honest with them. Be open and share. Share what it is that you want for your life. Other people might say, "I want that too. I want to go, please take me with you. I'll do whatever I have to do, I don't care what we're doing, I just want what you have right now, let's go." Those are the people you want to continue to hang around with and you want to influence them to go in that direction with you. Don't hang around those energy zombies or you are going to turn into one.

Let's take a look at the non-living things that you associate with in life. Do you associate with the television a lot? How about associating with a book instead. Do you associate with soda a lot? How about associating with water instead. Do you associate with the local bar? How about associating with the gym instead.

Your personal associations are going to be much harder to disassociate with because you are going to have a fear of hurting the feelings of the people who are your personal associations. It's a lot easier to disassociate with the things in your life. You can disassociate with a can of soda and you're not going to hurt its feelings. You can disassociate with the bar, right, but you might hurt the feelings of the people your disassociating with at the bar. Are you going to hurt the television's feelings if you read a book instead? Of course not, that's ridiculous. But you could hurt the feelings of the people who normally watch television with you. If your friends and the people you associate with are always going to the fast food restaurant for lunch and you don't want to eat fast food anymore because you want to have something healthy for lunch, what are you going to do? When they ask if you're going to lunch with them you could say, "Thanks so much for the invitation, I love going to lunch with you, but I just discovered this place next door to where we usually go and I tried their food and it's amazing. Would you guys want to go there today instead?" They might say yes, they might say no. If they say no you can just say, "okay, I'll catch up with you later, I'm going to go grab lunch from there." Learn to say no to others and say yes to yourself. If your friends are going to the bar for happy hour after work you can say, "Listen, I really love going to happy hour with you but I set a goal. I want to lose twenty pounds and I'm really focused on it right now." Whatever your motivation is, share it with them. Wish them a good time and stick to your goals.

Say no to those negative associations, and say yes to yourself. Identify those associations in your life right now. Make the choice to no longer allow those associations to hold you back from getting to where you want to be. You can't drag an energy zombie along with you when you're climbing toward the peak, that's exhausting. Much like time management, you need to be aware of how much the negative associations of life are affecting your ability to reach your goals.

Identify your positive and negative associations

Positive Associations

I will spend more time with

_____

I will spend more time with

_____

I will spend more time with

_____

I will spend more time with

_____

I will spend more time with

_____

Negative Associations

I will spend less time with

_____

I will spend less time with

_____

I will spend less time with

_____

I will spend less time with

_____

I will spend less time with

_____

Energy

Have you identified those energy zombies in your life, those people who are going to try to turn you into an energy zombie? Because it happens if you let it. Some of the people, in your life are going to be real energy drains. There are two things that happen at every moment of your life. The people, the places, and the things that you associate with are either going to energize you or they are going to drain your energy. They are either going to give you a power boost or they are going to drain your power. So you need to identify those things that are going to give you energy and you have to identify the things that are going to drain your energy.

That is what we are going to talk about right now, your energy. Now, we've talked about those energy zombies. They might be people dressed in plain clothes, they might have your last name, they might be living in your house, so be very careful because energy zombies can be really sneaky sometimes. Those energy zombies can drain your energy quickly. People who are negative all the time will typically drain your energy before you have the chance to increase theirs. People who are positive, smiling, outgoing, goal oriented, focused, those people give you energy. Energy zombies don't do those things. They don't smile a whole lot and they don't move a whole lot. They don't have a positive attitude and they don't use a whole lot of nice words. They don't give you energy.

Those places we talked about can also drain your energy. If you're at a bar, you are sitting there for hours talking to people who are probably energy zombies. I'm not saying they are, I'm just saying that the people that hang around a bar day in and day out might not be the people who are one hundred percent goal oriented and are going to move you forward. If that place is filled with negative people, even if you are associating with the positive people in your life, if you are associating with all the positive people in that negative space, the space itself is going to be an energy drain. Associate with those people at a different location. Influence them to go to the gym instead. Say, "Listen, I love hanging out with you but I have to tell you that those people at the bar are draining my energy. I have to get out of there. Do you want to start hitting the gym with me on Monday instead of the bar?" You will probably also find out that the money you were spending at the bar will pay for the gym membership!

Online groups and social networks can even drain your energy if the people on there are always complaining. If they are posting negative things, you are reading that stuff and it's going into your brain. It's influencing your thoughts and your feelings. You are being influenced, and that negativity can drain your energy.

How about what you are eating. Your nutrition is a primary source of energy as well as the exercise that you do. I am going to give you one simple way to recognize and to be more aware of the types of food that drain your energy. Now again, I'm not the type of person who is unrealistic about the types of food that you eat. You might be really dedicated to your nutrition and your exercise, and if so, that's great! You might be a person who is one hundred percent focused on health and that is your way of being in life, that's your primary goal, you want to be in the best shape of your life. If that is you, then you really need to focus heavily on your nutrition and your exercise. But if not, if you are just the person that says, "I want to have more energy in my life, how do I do that?" Well, it's not the energy drinks or the caffeinated beverages that are making a gazillion dollars right now because people think that's what gives them energy.

People are making the wrong choices when it comes to the nutrition they consume. It's very clear that the obesity epidemic is out of control. I heard recently that more people will die around the world from the effects of obesity than the effects of starvation. Isn't that awful? More people are going to die because they eat too much than those who don't have enough to eat. That's disturbing. Even if you just do a little research on nutrition, you'll be pretty shocked at some of the numbers. For instance, the average American consumes 150 pounds of refined sugar every year. That's nearly 3 pounds of sugar per week. General nutrition is a huge deal, but refined sugar intake is literally killing our society today. Refined sugar gives you no real sustainable energy and it produces a lack of motivation so people aren't moving enough. Those combinations are a killer. Now, here is my realistic and simple way of understanding what you should reduce in your diet. Again, I am not telling you to cut this stuff out completely but be aware of how often you are consuming it.

Your first energy drain is carbohydrates. Carbohydrates in general are not really the issue; it's the type of carbohydrates. We are a "bad carb" addicted society. Those foods which are high in calories, and low in nutrients, such as pasta, white bread, chips, pretzels and other cheap foods are an issue. There are two types of carbs, complex carbs, and simple carbs. You want to increase your intake of complex carbs and decrease your simple carbs. Whole grains, fruits, and vegetables are all complex carbs. They will help you energize your body.

Now the refined sugar that we spoke about can sneak up on you. One can of regular soda has about 150 calories. So if you have one can of regular soda per day, you are drinking 51,000 calories in a year because you are drinking just one soda per day. There are 39 grams of sugar in one can of soda. If you drink one can of soda per day then you are drinking 31 pounds of sugar in a year! Replace that one can of soda with water and you'll probably drop 15 pounds of excess weight from that alone this year. Refined sugar is all over the place. Do a little bit of research, again I'm not going to go into details about this, but do some research, watch your food labels and be aware of how sugar is adding up in your life.

Now, what about alcohol? Alcohol is an energy drain but it is also a motivation killer. You can be really into doing something, have a drink and you don't want to do it anymore. I'm not telling you not to drink alcohol again, I'm not that kind of a coach. I'm not the kind of person that says, you need to cut this out of your life completely because that's why you are not achieving your goals. That is probably not true, but the amount of alcohol that you are having may be affecting your life. So just reduce it and disassociate from the alcohol. If you want to achieve more in your life, you have to make these changes.

What about processed foods and especially fast food? The amount of saturated fats in fast food is astounding. If you find yourself eating fast food a lot, be aware that there are healthier food options out there. I get it, kids love fast food. Kids love to stop at McDonald's and eat that stuff but you don't have to stop there and, if you do, you don't have to get yourself something to eat there. You can wait until you get home or you can stop somewhere else. You're driving the car. You make the choice and you influence what happens to you and your family and what they eat. Always be sure you have a snack handy or that you eat before leaving the house so you are not tempted by the fast food restaurants while you are out.

How are you going to remember all of this? Simple. Cut the crap! Cut the crap out of your life! Reduce it. Crap...C.R.A.P...Carbs, Refined sugar, Alcohol, and Processed foods. Cut the crap out of your life and it will increase your energy. The nutrition training within the LifeTrax Success System allows you to track your nutrition. You can be more aware of what you are eating and drinking and it will have a drastic effect on the energy that you have. You will be amazed when you start to keep track of what you are consuming, the calories, the fat, the sugar, whatever you keep track of, when that starts to add up you'll say, "Wow, I had no idea." You can learn more about the health coaching I provide at LifeTrax.com and contact me if I can help you in any way. All of our fitness and nutrition products are the best available.

Of course if your nutrition is better and you're losing weight and you start to feel healthier, that is going to have a drastic effect on your self-confidence. When you have more self-confidence, you have more of a desire to do things in your life. There are many benefits to increasing and improving your nutrition. If you need to have a lot of help in this area, I'm not the right guy. But there are lots of licensed nutritionists, who are focused on, licensed and committed to helping you in that area of your life. So if you seriously need to look at how you can change your life from a nutrition and exercise standpoint then hire a nutritionist specifically for that purpose.

There is so much information out there but just monitor where you are getting the information. Make sure they are credible sources but most of all seek out the information and take action on what you learn. The one thing I want you to understand above everything else is that the nutrition in food is the energy you use to fuel your body. It is not the thing you use to fill an emotional void because you felt like you didn't get enough love as a kid so you turned to food as a comfort. That is nothing more than a thought. That thought is something you have allowed yourself to believe. Energy comes from food. You use that food to fuel your body. If you have an emotional void that is due to something else that happened in your life, well then get some help with that, get some help identifying what that is. This book might help you to do that, but don't use food as an excuse because there is an answer and food is not it.

Exercise is something that can be done to boost your energy as well. We talked about this a little when we talked about consistency. Those 30 pushups a day add up to 10,950 pushups over a year. That's an astounding amount of pushups. What if you were to just do 30 second bursts of exercise. We live in a society that wants everything now. People want to get rich quick by simply buying a program. People want to lose weight by sitting on the magical butt-shrinking chair. Your situation doesn't magically change that way. You have to do the work consistently. You have to focus, dedicate yourself, and be committed to your goals. How do you do that if you're just starting to figure out how you can incorporate all the things that you have been learning into your life? Maybe you're embarrassed to go to the gym. I'm not going to tell you that 30 second bursts is the best way to lose weight and get fit, but it will help.

Home based fitness programs are great at teaching you how to find some exercises that you can do during those times when you aren't doing anything else. Those times when you pop something in the microwave and stand there waiting, find a body weight exercise that you can do during those times. We have tons of home fitness videos available at LifeTrax.com. You can watch the previews and figure out which program will work for you, or contact me and I will help you decide on the perfect program for you.

Fill in those little gaps in your time during the day and keep your heart rate elevated all day long by doing short bursts of exercise if that works for you. Again, I'm not going to tell you doing 30 minutes of a high intensity workout several days a week isn't going to help you more. But if you are trying to figure out how you can fit exercise into your life, this is a great way to do it. Then when your energy increases and you find that you can wake up earlier so you can do a more focused program because you have more energy, and you are using your time management more effectively, then that's a great way to continue reaching toward your goal. Going to the gym is also a great way to surround yourself with people who are energy boosters. You might find some people who are moving in the same direction as you. Make some friends with the people at the gym. Find out what they are up to in their life. You might find someone who is going in the same direction you are going and you can support each other and get there together. Surround yourself with people who are motivated and you will become more motivated.

So, monitor your nutrition and find time to do some exercise. Even if you are just making little changes in your life to start out, the changes that will happen over a longer period of time will make an incredible impact in your life. I am a health and wellness coach, so if you want some help in this area, please reach out to me.

Increase your energy through nutrition

Increase the positive

I will eat healthier by eating more

_____

I will eat healthier by eating more

_____

I will eat healthier by eating more

_____

I will eat healthier by eating more

_____

I will eat healthier by eating more

_____

Decrease the negative

I will eat healthier by eating less

_____

I will eat healthier by eating less

_____

I will eat healthier by eating less

_____

I will eat healthier by eating less

_____

I will eat healthier by eating less

_____

Increase your energy through exercise

How can you move more in your life?

I will move more by doing

_____

I will move more by doing

_____

I will move more by doing

_____

I will move more by doing

_____

I will move more by doing

_____

How can you exercise more in your life?

I will exercise more by doing

_____

I will exercise more by doing

_____

I will exercise more by doing

_____

I will exercise more by doing

_____

I will exercise more by doing

_____

Expectations, Commitments, Integrity

What are our expectations? Well there are two different kinds. There are expectations you have of yourself and then there are the expectations you have of other people. What do you expect from yourself? Do you expect yourself to get up at a certain time every day and achieve a certain amount of goals every day? Do you expect yourself to exercise for a certain amount of time? Do you expect yourself to eat a certain way? Do you expect yourself to speak in a certain way? Do you expect yourself to be happy? Do you expect yourself to be open minded? Do you expect yourself to share openly? Do you expect to fail or do you expect to win? Do you expect that after you do something over a certain period of time that you will probably give up? Your expectations of yourself are a huge factor in your success. What you expect you typically get.

Now, what do you expect from other people? Do you expect people to not like you? Do you expect other people to influence your thoughts? Do you expect other people to like you? Do you expect other people to respect you? Do you expect other people to honor your requests? What do you expect from other people? If you expect people to behave a certain way and they continue to not live up to those expectations, how long are you going to put up with those inconsistencies in your life? How long are you going to put up with broken expectations from someone else in your life?

The first place you have to start with your expectations is your expectations of yourself. You need to be able to expect yourself to do what you said you would do when you said you would do it. When you do what you said you would do, when and how you said you would do it, that's integrity. You need to expect yourself to live with integrity. You also need to expect yourself to be committed.

Commitment is doing what you said you would do long after the mood you said it in has disappeared. Think of marriage when you think of commitment. What's the definition again? Doing what you said you would do long after the mood you said it in has disappeared. So what happens? People go to the altar and they say "I Do." When they say I Do they are in a mood. They are in a happy, loving, giving mood. They say, "I Do, I will honor you, I will commit to you, I will live with you and we will have our hard times but we will be together until death do us part. I Do." Then what happens? Time goes by, the mood changes, things get tough, the tough things start to build up, maybe you argue, you run into some of life's challenges and the mood you said it in has long been forgotten. That's why people get divorced, because they don't do what they said they would do long after the mood they said it in has been forgotten. When they said 'I Do' they were in a mood, once they get into a fight and they continue to have more challenges in life, that mood is gone. So if their commitment was 'I do until death do us part' and they don't honor that commitment, divorce happens. It's a great way to look at commitment.

Now, trust me, when you're married or in a relationship or

anything you are committed to, you are going to have challenges that change your mood. Nonetheless, no matter what you commit to, if you honor that commitment to yourself, your life gets easier. When you expect more from yourself, and you honor your commitments, life gets easier. Like I have said before, living a life of integrity is simple but it's not easy. There is a huge difference between simple and easy. Doing what you said you would do long after the mood you said it in is simple if you follow what we are talking about here, but it's not easy. Living with integrity, doing what you said you would do, when and how you said you would do it, is simple but it's not easy. But when you practice being true to your commitments and acting with integrity more and more in your life, then your life will get easier.

Make sure the people around you are holding you to the level of expectations that you want them to hold you to. Don't allow them to let you off the hook. If you said, "I'm going to do this" and you don't honor that commitment, have them call you out on it, and don't make excuses, own it. Say, "You know what, you're right, I did not honor my commitment, I did not live with integrity, and I am committed to living a life of commitment and integrity and I apologize because I was not living up to my expectations of myself. I am working really hard on living that kind of a life and you are absolutely right, I did not honor that commitment and I am going to continue to work on it. I can't change what I did but I can make you the commitment again and I am going to continue to work on honoring my commitments." That's all you can do.

Here is what I want to warn you about. I want to warn you of your expectations in relation to how you think other people should act, behave, and react. Because when you have an expectation of how you think other people should behave, you might be horribly disappointed. You cannot control other people. You can influence other people but you cannot control other people. You can influence other people forcefully but they are not going to like it. So don't have unrealistic expectations of other people. You will never be able to control what other people do, say, feel, or anything else over the long term. It can be done over a short term, possibly. A cop could force someone into a car because they are in handcuffs but in your life you cannot and should not force someone to do something that they may not yet be ready to do. You can only influence people to live in a way that you would like to see them live. You can't force people to do anything and have it be a mutually agreeable act.

Here is the best way to live your life when it comes to your expectations of commitment and integrity. From yourself, expect 100% commitment and integrity. Live your own life in that way and you will influence those around you to live with more commitment and integrity. If they are not living their life in the way you want to be associated with, make the choice of whether or not to continue the relationship. Discuss with them how you would like to see them behave and allow them to either live in that way, or not. Unless you clarify your expectations of them, the people in your life will not know what you expect. Once the expectation is set, it's up to them to meet the expectations or not and it's up to you to adjust your life accordingly.

Honor your commitments and set your expectations

Honor your commitments

I am committing to

_____

I am committing to

_____

I am committing to

_____

I am committing to

_____

I am committing to

_____

Set your expectations

I expect myself to

_____

I expect myself to

_____

I expect myself to

_____

I expect myself to

_____

I expect myself to

_____

Put Yourself First

Who is the most important person in your life? Is it your children, is it your spouse, is it your parents, or is it your significant other? Who is the most important person in your life? You are! You are the most important person in your life. If you are giving up everything that you want in your life so that other people can have what they want in their life, you are not honoring your commitment to being the most important person in your life. You are the most important person in your life. Other people come in really close behind you, but you are number one.

If you are a parent, I know that you would give your life for your children. That's not the kind of, you're more important than they are scenario that I'm talking about here. But when it comes to who you are honoring your commitments to, who you are being honest with, who you are living a life of integrity for, who do you need to do that for the most? You need to do it for you. When you focus on you, everything around you will begin to improve. When you focus and improve on how you are being and what you are doing, everything around you will begin to improve. When you focus on getting done what you need to get done then everything around you will improve. When you focus on how you are speaking, everyone else will begin to speak in a better way.

When you say no to other people, you say yes to yourself. Creating your life is your responsibility. You must look at yourself as the root cause of your life. If your ideal life is living in a way that spending time with your children is everything to you, then you have to create your life in a way that allows you to live a life that is one hundred percent dedicated to your children. If you want to dedicate your time to your kids because you know that having a relationship with them is important, but you are sacrificing time with them for other things in your life, you are going to live with regret. Living a life that you want to live is putting yourself first. Figure out how you can control your time, your energy, and your thoughts, so that you can focus on creating the life that you want to live. You always need to focus on you, because if you're not then you are living your life in the exact opposite way that you need to live. You are going to focus on the outside instead of on the inside. You're living your life from the outside in when you are supposed to be living your life from the inside out. This may sound selfish to you right now, but read on because I want you to learn how to put yourself first so you can actually give more of yourself to the people in your life.

I saved what I told you I was going to do earlier until this section. Remember, I told you that I was going to show you how to create time? How to literally create as much time as you want in your life? How to create 6 days of time this year if you want 6 days or if you want 30 days then how to create 30 days? I'm going to show you how to do that. We did the math for things that add up to a significant amount of time in your life during the time management section but right now we are talking about putting you first; putting your goals first. We are going to talk about putting you ahead of anything else in your life. So that's why this section is perfect for talking about how to create time.

In the time management section, we talked about how two hours of television a day adds up to 30 days of time over a year. So if you need a month to accomplish your goal, are you going to be able to take an entire month, not eat, not sleep, not go to the bathroom, not take any phone calls, not have any interruptions, and have one hundred percent focus on your goal? Are you going to be able to stay awake for 30 days straight? No, of course not. So how do you create those 30 days? You focus. You focus on your goal instead of focusing on the tv. You take two hours each day for one year and you focus on your goal instead of whatever else you are using the same 2 hours for each day. The time doesn't change, your priority changes. Where were you last year at this exact time. Has your life drastically changed? I bet if you had taken those two hours every day and instead of watching tv or doing whatever it is that's taking you two hours to do, and you focused on your goal of being whatever you want to be last year, your life would be completely different today. If you begin to focus on doing whatever you want to do, or having whatever you want to have, if you took those two hours every single day and focused on your goals this year, you would give yourself 30 days of time this year. Do the math, you'll see. Next year when I check in with you and say, "How is your life going? Did you use those two hours every day to focus on your goals? Has your life drastically changed this year?" I bet you that your answer is "Yes!"

Now what if you don't need 30 days of time, what if you only have some small goals that you want to achieve, that's okay too. Listen, you don't have to change the world. I'm not telling you to go out there and influence the entire world. Different people want different things. I want you to do what is important to you. So what if you just need 6 days of time. Well, how about this, what would happen if you were to wake up 1 hour earlier, three days a week? Let's just say Monday, Wednesday, and Friday, you woke up one hour before you usually do and you took that hour and you focused on accomplishing your goal. If you did one hour, three days a week for a year, that's six and a half days of time you create this year. So I've even given you a half a day that you can say, "I don't feel like doing it." However, I hope you don't do that because that's doing what? That's not honoring your commitments and that's not living with integrity. When you don't live with commitment and integrity, your life is going to be harder. So figure it out, do the math. It's pretty awesome when you do the math and see that if you just take one hour here and one hour there and consistently put it towards what you want to achieve, then in one year what would that add up to? You will be blown away.

Why do I talk about integrity and commitment so much? Because a lot of people struggle with those two things. I can teach you how to create time, but you have to be committed to actually get out of bed and do it. I can show you where to increase your effectiveness, but you have to live with integrity in order for it to make a difference. The only thing that will make change happen in your life is taking action on what you said you would do. So if you plan to get up and work on your goals, do it! If you say you will dedicate a certain time to your goals, do it! It's a practice, like anything else, and once you begin living this way, it will become a positive addiction! Become addicted to creating time and getting things done. We were not made to waste our time on earth.

So I hope now you can see that is why I don't allow you to use time as an excuse. I'm pretty sure that if you were to look around at how you were living your daily life, you would say, I can see where I can find some time here. People always ask me "Where do you find the time to do everything you do?" I've just told you my secret! Committing, having a purpose for your time and living with integrity. That is how you create time.

Intuition

What is your intuition? Your intuition or what you may think of as your instincts, are like a quick vision into your future. It's that gut feeling you get that you know you shouldn't ignore. Intuition allows you to make a decision on what you should or shouldn't do and what you need to do in the moment or not do in the moment. Once you make the decision, based on your intuition, you can make the choice on what you are going to do and then you take action. You need to learn to recognize that intuition and to learn to recognize those moments of should and shouldn't. The more in tune you become to your intuition, based on what you want, the faster you will begin to see positive life changes happen.

We all have a lot of moments in our lives when we said, "I should have done that," and other moments when you said, "I shouldn't have done that." Those are the ways we look back at the choices we made when we had an intuition. When you have an intuition, you are going to be faced with making a decision. Intuitions can be small things. You might have an intuition that says, "I should grab my phone before I head to the store" but you dishonor that intuition and leave it on the counter. On your way to the store, you witness an accident, reach for your phone to call 911 but it's not there. That's an intuition, that's a thought. If I make this decision, that might happen, if I make that decision, this might happen. Learn to be aware of your intuition and take the small actions necessary to honor those intuitions.

When you have an intuition you are making a decision and you are running through your mind the different scenarios that may occur based on your decision. What you need to do is recognize and make an educated, and intuitive decision in the moment of how you should handle that sixth sense. You're going to have times when your intuition is going to tell you to do one thing and you're going to think, "Whew, that was wrong, that didn't work out the way I thought it was going to." Then you will have other times when you say, "I'm so thankful that I did that because that intuition was one hundred percent right on." The reality though is that we never know what will happen in the future. So, something that may seem like it was not the right idea immediately, may have long term benefits. Conversely, something that seems like a short term benefit, may have long term implications.

Intuitions can also be larger. You may get a gut feeling like a relationship is not right for you. Once again, we just don't always know how today's decision will influence tomorrow's outcome. However, I encourage you to follow your heart as well as using logic and reason to determine how you respond to your intuition.

So what should you do when you have the thought, "What should I do?" Ask yourself "Will this take me closer to or further away from where I want to be?" When your intuition is talking to you, acknowledge it! Realize you are seeing a glimpse into your future. We can't predict our future, but we can influence our future. If you make one choice it's going to affect your life in one way, if you make another choice it's going to affect your life in a different way.

So the way that you recognize and follow your intuitions and keep your choices in line with what you want for your life is to ask yourself that question. "Will this take me closer to or further away from what I want?"

To clarify what I mean, using the previous examples, you can think of it this way. If your intuition says "Grab the phone," and your goal is too always be prepared, then don't ignore that intuition. If your intuition says "This person isn't going to support me the way I want to be supported in a relationship" then talk to them about what you need. Recognizing intuition and being intuitive is all about anticipating what might happen based upon your own experiences and combining that with an unexplainable guiding voice.

When I talk about intuitions and making a decision and a choice, you probably hear me using both words. I want to show you the difference so that you understand the distinction between the two words. Decisions are something that you make in your own mind on a constant and ongoing basis. Decisions don't really have much to do with how our life goes. We can go back and forth, time and again, and make decision after decision. That, technically, would be considered indecision. Your decisions don't really affect your life.

With that being said, we don't have choice without decision. So in that case, decision is actually the only thing that sets us apart from other instinctual beings. All other creatures act on instinct. They have limited to no decisions making capabilities. As humans, our choice is what affects our life. If you choose one decision, life moves in a certain direction. Choose another decision, life moves in the opposite direction. Don't ever make a choice, and life doesn't change at all. Life direction occurs at the moment of choice. When you make a choice, you take action.

C.H.O.I.C.E.

I want to talk to you specifically about the six most important things you must choose to do and be in order to achieve your goals. When you make the decision about what you want in your life, what are the six things that you are going to have to do in order to be successful? No matter what you want, these six elements won't change.

You are going to have to make the choice to be consistent. This is the hardest part of achieving your goals. Many people can start and stop and start and stop but very few people can be consistent. That requires a relentless determination. Determination is generally based on your reason why. If you have a strong reason why you are doing something, consistency becomes much easier. The first and hardest part of achieving your goals is consistency. You must make the choice to be consistent in life. Make consistent choices that are in line with what you want. Take consistent actions that are in line with what you want.

The second hardest thing to be when achieving your goals is honest. You are going to need to be honest with yourself. You're going to have to say, "I'm not being honest with myself about my time management. I'm not being honest with myself about my nutrition. I'm not being honest with myself about my associations." You need to be honest not only with yourself but you need to be honest with the other people in your life. You need to be able to say to them what you do want and what you don't want. You need to be honest about what is important in your life. Honesty is not always an easy thing but when you make the choice to live the life that you want to live, honesty is very, very important. So you need to work on that and you need to make the choice to be honest.

The third hardest thing to be is open. You have to be open in your mind. Having an open mind about what is possible in your life is incredibly important. You have to be open to opportunities that arise in your life. Remember, the moments of your life are opportunities. You have to be open with the people in your life. You need to be open to conversation and you need to be open to changes. Openness allows you to let things into your life. Openness also allows you to let things go.

For example, when you open your arms you allow someone to give you a hug. When you open yourself up emotionally then you allow people into your life. When you have an open mind then you allow new thoughts to flow in. When you have an open heart you allow love to come in. So openness is very important and it is something that you have to practice. It's not easy, but openness is simple. You need to make the choice to be open.

Now the fourth thing that you should work on once you make a choice to achieve your goals is integrity. Living with integrity is really important to your success. You need to do what you said you would do, when and how you said you would do it, not only for yourself but for other people. If people are expecting you to do something and you don't do it, then what does that say to them? It says that you are unreliable. People want to be able to rely on you. So make the choice to live with integrity. The more people can rely on you, the more they will call on you. If you want to be desired, be desirable. A man or woman of integrity in every area of their life is a very desirable person.

The fifth thing is being committed. Doing what you said you would do long after the mood you said it in has disappeared. You need to make the choice to honor your commitments. You are going to have to make the choice that you are not going to allow the things that get in the way in your life to stop you from living the life that you want to live. You need to be committed, so choose commitment in your life. This will likely require you to sacrifice and make some tough decisions. Being committed to something is powerful! When you are committed, you let nothing and no one stand in your way.

The final thing is energy. You need to choose to have energy in your life. You need to choose energy boosters. Maintain your energy through your thoughts and maintain your energy because you are motivated by your reason why. Make the choice to fill your body with energy producing foods. Make the choice to have the energy that you need in your life. Remember, at any moment, what you are doing is likely energizing you or draining your energy. Be acutely aware of your energy and how it is affecting your ability to succeed.

Let's review them again. By this point you know that I like word play. Think of the letters in the word CHOICE in order to make the choices that are important to achieving your goals and living the life that you want to live. C, consistency, you need to make the choice to be consistent. H, honesty, you need to make the choice to be honest. O, openness, you need to make the choice to be open in your life, open minded, open hearted, open to conversation, open to change. I, integrity, you have to make the choice to live with integrity. C, commitment, you have to make a choice that you are making a commitment. Finally E, energy, you have to make the choice to generate energy, so you have the energy that you need to get to where you want to go. If the car that you are driving doesn't have the energy it needs to get to where you want to go because you didn't put the gas in the car, you are not going to get there, so choose to have energy.

Choice. C H O I C E: Consistency, Honesty, Openness, Integrity, Commitment, and Energy.

Make the right choices.

When (what happens)_____
I will _____

When (what happens)_____
I will _____

When (what happens)_____
I will _____

When (what happens)_____
I will _____

When (what happens)_____
I will _____

When (what happens)_____
I will _____

When (what happens)_____
I will _____

When (what happens)_____
I will _____

When (what happens)_____
I will _____

Create Your Goal

So, let's go create a goal. The whole point to this entire book was to help you learn how to accomplish one goal. Now, I could have really easily taught you the very basics of goal setting but I know that there are a lot of other elements that go into achieving your goals consistently in your life. Again, I didn't say that I was going to help you learn how to set a goal. I said I was going to teach you how to achieve your goals. Once you learn how to achieve one goal, then you can achieve another goal, and another goal, and another goal after that. You can set bigger and better goals and then envision possibilities for yourself bigger then you have ever imagined in your life.

In just a couple of minutes, you will turn to the pages where you can put all of this new knowledge into action. Remember, I said in the beginning that if you just read this book, you will gain knowledge, but if you do the work, you can transform your life! This book is designed to help you in the most efficient way possible. First, you will learn the information, and then you will do the work.

Right now I want you to identify a single goal for yourself. What are you going to do, specifically? What exactly are you going to do in your life? This could be a very small goal but you have to make it important to you, which brings me to my next point. Why are you motivated to work on this goal? What is motivating you? What is your reason why? Write down your reason why, write down your specific goal, and write down specific steps. Again, use all the tools and information you've learned in this book to take action. Just follow the instructions and you will create your goal. We want to achieve the first step of simply creating your goal to get into momentum. Next, commit to doing what you say you are going to do. How long is it going to take you to achieve this goal? Are you going to do it in a week, in a month, in a year, in ten years? I'm hoping you are going to commit to something that is more of a short term goal, because remember short term goals accomplished over a period of time equal long term goals accomplished. So when are you going to commit to doing this. Exactly when during the day are you going to commit to doing it?

Here is how you can use this information together. Take the step from your goal and copy that step and write it into your "to do list." Then take that step and set a date and time when you are going to accomplish that goal. Put yourself first. You've dedicated that time and you've committed to accomplishing that step. Do it, do it for you. Lastly, keep moving until you have reached your desired result. Mark off your steps. Allow those little checkmarks to motivate you. If you find yourself getting stopped at any point, just ask yourself, "What would I have to believe in order not to keep going? What would my belief system have to be in order for me to not take consistent action in order to get what I want?" Answer that question for yourself and then change your belief and decide what you would have to 'be, do, or have' to keep going and complete that step or to achieve that goal.

If your belief is not empowering you, use the affirmation tools, create new affirmations, and create a new belief system for yourself. Be aware of who is going to be involved in this? Do you need to talk to some people in your life? Who is involved with this goal? What and who are your associations? What do you need to cut out of your life and what do you need to include into your life? Who are the people, what are the places and things that will either reduce your energy or increase your energy? I want you to focus on the things that are going to increase your energy.

Now, I hope by this point that you can see how achieving your goals is actually quite simple. I hope that this book has allowed you to see how you can begin to create your life. As we continue with the rest of this series, we are moving on to what's called The Next Level. In my next book, The Next Level, we are really going to identify specifically what is going to attempt to stop you from reaching the peak. There are four things that are going to do their best to block you from achieving what you want to achieve in your life. What you want in your life lies just beyond those four things.

Before you move on to The Next Level, I'm going to ask that you set, and then achieve one goal for yourself. Show yourself that achieving your goals is possible. Watch how each of the elements that were discussed in this first book come into play. It doesn't have to be a huge goal but accomplish something for yourself and then once you do that, I want you to say to yourself, "It really is possible to live the life I want. It really is possible to achieve my goals." Once you have achieved your first goal then I'd encourage you to read The Next Level. The Next Level is an extraordinary book. In The Next Level we are going to spend a lot of time in your head. I'm going to get in there and poke around a little bit. I'm going to allow you to see what's holding you back, and that is an extraordinary experience. When you get done with The Next Level, your view of life, of people, of how you think, of how other people think, and what you understand about life itself is going to be at a whole new level.

I hope you have enjoyed learning the ABC's Of Success. Again, these are the fundamentals, and this is what we are going to build upon. What you just learned is everything you need to take you to The Next Level but it's not everything you need to create the life that you want. This is the foundation. If you don't have these, you probably aren't going to reach the point at which you say to yourself, "I've got everything that I want in my life." So practice these fundamentals. Use the following pages to review what you learned, and write down what you want. Bring your new life into existence! Now, please, go out there and accomplish your goal and I'll see you at The Next Level.

Create your goals

Goal 1

Specifically, I am going to

_____

_____

I am going to do this because (my why)

_____

_____

The steps I will take are

_____

_____

_____

_____

I am committed to achieving this goal by (date/time)

_____

"I will stay committed, I will keep going, and I will achieve this goal! I might mess up, but I will not give up!"

Goal 2

Specifically, I am going to

_____

_____

I am going to do this because (my why)

_____

_____

The steps I will take are

_____

_____

_____

_____

I am committed to achieving this goal by (date/time)

_____

"I will stay committed, I will keep going, and I will achieve this goal! I might mess up, but I will not give up!"

Goal 3

Specifically, I am going to

_____

_____

I am going to do this because (my why)

_____

_____

The steps I will take are

_____

_____

_____

_____

I am committed to achieving this goal by (date/time)

_____

"I will stay committed, I will keep going, and I will achieve this goal! I might mess up, but I will not give up!"

Goal 4

Specifically, I am going to

_____

_____

I am going to do this because (my why)

_____

_____

The steps I will take are

_____

_____

_____

_____

I am committed to achieving this goal by (date/time)

_____

"I will stay committed, I will keep going, and I will achieve this goal! I might mess up, but I will not give up!"

Goal 5

Specifically, I am going to

_____

_____

I am going to do this because (my why)

_____

_____

The steps I will take are

_____

_____

_____

_____

I am committed to achieving this goal by (date/time)

_____

"I will stay committed, I will keep going, and I will achieve this goal! I might mess up, but I will not give up!"

Time to reflect

It's time to reflect on where you were, how far you've come, and then project where you are going. When you started your journey of being, you may have found yourself in a pretty dark place. You may have been in a place you never want to go back to, in fact, I'm hoping you were. Because being able to look back in retrospect helps us to understand why we had to go through what we did. I love the saying that goes, "Life can only be lived moving ahead, but it only makes sense looking back."

So you're probably wondering, what now? I have all these goals, I am motivated, and I am ready to change my life. However, I've been here before, and I've felt this way at times, but I usually fall off track, and find myself back where I was when I started this journey.

Well, I have great news for you. This is not the end of this journey, it's literally just the beginning. Besides having written several other books which will continue to keep you on track, moving forward, and propelling your life in the direction you want it to go, I offer coaching in various forms as well.

The next book in this series is called, Your Journey Of Being – The Next Level. In the next level, you will learn mindset principles that will allow you to overcome that negative voice in your head, every time it talks to you. You will discover how to power through any obstacles that are slowing you down right now. You will, and I say this with conviction, be living your life at a whole new level of strength, clarity, and personal influence when you finish that book.

There is an old saying that goes, "Even if you're on the right track, you'll get run over if you just sit there." So don't allow yourself to sit still, get up, get out of your own way, and allow The Next Level to propel you toward the peak! There are always new realms of possibility, new heights to reach, new perspectives to discover, and new places to explore.

One of my mentors, Eric Worre once said, "I'm going to the top! You're either going to find me dead on the side, or waving from the top, because I'm NOT coming back!"

Now who's coming with me?

About the author

Tom Anderson is a passionate entrepreneur who loves helping people identify their life purpose, and then inspire, motivate, and empower them to live fully, boldly, and outrageously focused on what matters to them with the one life they have to live.

His focus is on helping people improve every area of their life, by specifically focusing on showing others how to live happier, more rewarding lives, by discovering and fulfilling their God given purpose in life.

If you'd like to speak directly with Tom, contact him at his websites, LifeTrax.com, or The Purpose Guy.com

Made in the USA
Charleston, SC
09 December 2016